The Pastor's Wife Today

Donna Sinclair

Creative Leadership Series
Lyle E. Schaller, Editor

Abingdon / Nashville

THE PASTOR'S WIFE TODAY

Copyright © 1981 by Abingdon

Library of Congress Cataloging in Publication Data

SINCLAIR, DONNA, 1943–
   The pastor's wife today.
   (Creative leadership series)
   Bibliography: p.
   1. Clergymen's wives. I. Title. II. Series.
   BV4395.S56   253'.2   80-26076

ISBN 0-687-30269-2

The epigraph on page 60 is excerpted from "The Good Little Girl" from
NOW WE ARE SIX by A. A. Milne. Copyright, 1927, by E. P. Dutton &
Co., Inc. Renewal, 1955, by A. A. Milne. Reprinted by permission of the
publisher, E. P. Dutton; by permission of The Canadian Publishers,
McClelland and Stewart Limited, Toronto; and by permission of
Methuen Children's Books Ltd., London.

MANUFACTURED BY THE PARTHENON PRESS AT
NASHVILLE, TENNESSEE, UNITED STATES OF AMERICA

The Pastor's Wife Today

Creative Leadership Series

To Patricia Clarke
and James Taylor,
with thanks

Overheard in the playroom: David (age four) encouraging Andy (age two) with a painting:
David: What's it going to be, Andy?
Andy: It's something *now!*

Foreword

A long, long time ago on what, to many of us who were born during the first third of the twentieth century, was another planet in a different galaxy, a lady wrote a book directed to women who were married to Protestant ministers. That author was Carolyn P. Blackwood and she completed the book, *The Pastor's Wife* (Westminster Press, 1951), after forty years of marriage to the Reverend Doctor Andrew W. Blackwood, one of the most widely known authorities on the pastoral ministry during the middle third of this century. It was a good book. It was filled with very practical advice for the woman married to a minister back in 1910 or 1920 or 1930 or 1940 or 1950. The world of the minister's wife in 1950 closely resembled the world that other ministers' wives had inhabited a decade or two or three or four earlier.

Mrs. Blackwood's book was directed, to use Donna Sinclair's system of classification, to those women who were filling the role of the minister's "helpmate." The book strongly affirmed that traditional role. Mrs. Blackwood emphasized such concepts as courtesy, carriage, neatness, and cheerfulness. She lifted up the importance of protecting the husband and his time, of setting an example of gracious living on a modest income, of being able and willing to entertain church officials in the parsonage or manse and of being a cheerleader who encouraged her husband to go on to victory. One chapter in the book (remember, it was published in 1951) described the role of the pastor's wife as a financial expert who could make ends meet on an annual cash salary of $2,500—of which $225 was allocated to utilities, $275 went for automobile expenses, and the first $250 was reserved for contributions to religious causes. The importance of the large garden in the backyard of the manse was described in economic terms, not as a vehicle for the release of emotions.

In her book Mrs. Blackwood dealt at length with the role of the minister's wife in working with other women and the women's organization in the church, with the importance of calling on members in their homes, and on being a living example of a committed Christian woman.

Just as the first quarter of the twentieth century served as a part of the prologue for today's world, Carolyn Blackwood's description of the role of the pastor's wife serves as a beginning point for a contemporary examination of the same subject. But that common beginning point of the concept of the "helpmate" also marks the beginning of the differences between these two books. Carolyn Blackwood described a static role for the minister's wife. Donna Sinclair uses a more dynamic frame of reference and describes a pilgrimage. Mrs. Blackwood wrote largely in terms of the functions that accompany the role of minister's wife. Mrs. Sinclair writes from a relational perspective.

Mrs. Blackwood's account was written in an impersonal, professional, functional, descriptive, and success-oriented style that was very appropriate for the first half of this century. Mrs. Sinclair's story is highly personal, autobiographical, relational, and is as much concerned with failures and near failures as it is with victories. It is a story that would not have been written fifty years ago because it could not have been written. Mrs. Blackwood describes how a minister's wife can be successful and effective in filling a role that has been defined for her. Mrs. Sinclair writes about the importance of seeing life as a journey and of the growth that can come from moving from one stage of adult development to a new stage. She emphasizes the importance of choosing to grow and to change rather than trying to fit into a role defined by someone else. Mrs. Blackwood assumed the alternatives open to a pastor's wife were basically success and failure. Mrs. Sinclair assumes a far wider range of choices are now available to the woman married to a pastor.

Mrs. Blackwood wrote from a world that was filled with "shoulds!" while Mrs. Sinclair writes from a perspective that is filled with "whys?" Mrs. Blackwood's world was marked by an acceptance of the value of stability while Mrs. Sinclair's world is distinguished by a growing recognition of the value of change.

To a remarkable degree these two books reflect the changes in society and in the religious culture that have occurred on the North American continent since the close of World War II. These two books also illustrate many of the changes that have taken place in only three decades in the role of women in Western society.

Despite the differences, and they are as different as the point of view of a grandmother often is from the perspective of her mature granddaughter, there are many, many parallels in these two books. Both authors repeatedly affirm the writer's relationship with her minister-husband. Both affirm the centrality of the family. Both express their gratitude for the support of the community of faith. Both emphasize the importance of prayer. Both recognize the unique gifts that accompany motherhood. Both represent a strong commitment to the Christian church. When read together these two books remind us that while some things change radically, other things remain the same from generation to generation.

This book, by the wife of a minister in the United Church of Canada, should have a special appeal to other women who also are married to clergymen and who want to reflect on their own pilgrimage from within the context of someone else's journey. It should be of deep interest to lay leaders who are interested in learning more about how the world looks from the perspective of the minister's wife. It will be a revealing study for many teen-agers and young adults of the last part of this century who seek a better understanding of their mother's pilgrimage. It also may gain the attention of some of the thousands of ministers who, years ago, married the congregation they serve and who recently have begun to wonder whatever happened to that "helpmate" they married a decade or two ago. Those readers will understand why this volume belongs in a series that is directed at "Creative Leaders."

Lyle E. Schaller
Yokefellow Institute
Richmond, Indiana

Acknowledgments

This book has been underway (off and on) for two years. My husband Jim and our two boys, David and Andy, have been unfailingly supportive, as have my parents, who cheerfully took me and the baby in whenever I needed a study leave.

Many women have gladly given their time to discuss the contents of this book, especially the women of the Yamaska Valley Women's Group, in Quebec's Eastern Townships, and the various divorced women (formerly pastors' wives) who helped me with chapter 4.

St. Paul's United Church in Schefferville, Emmanuel in Cowansville, and St. Andrew's in North Bay have strengthened my faith and encouraged my belief that the local congregation is a uniquely powerful instrument for the expression of God's love.

Bob Shorten provided material and support generously.

The "Insearch" seminars at Five Oaks, led by Russ

Becker, provided many of the ideas found here; especially for chapters two and three.

Betty Hurley typed this. Ann Myers babysat Tracy. I'm thankful for the concern each of them showed for my various offspring.

And Lyle Schaller proved that it is possible to be a superb pastor, by mail.

I am extremely grateful to all these people.

Contents

Introduction

When I first began to write this book, I found myself surrounded with paper a good deal of the time. It seemed to have a life of its own, accumulating wherever I sat down. One night I had crawled into bed, accompanied by my mounds of yellow foolscap, and was joined by my six-year-old, attempting to crawl in for a bedtime snuggle. His space, however, was completely filled with books and papers.

"What are you doing, Mom, with all that paper?"

"Well, I'm writing a book, Andy."

"What about?"

"About what it's like being a lady, I guess. And married to Daddy."

"That's weird, Mom. *Weird.*"

"How come?"

"Well, only men are going to buy your book, you know. Not girls and women."

"How come?"

"'Cause girls and women already *know* what it's like, being a lady. Why should *they* read the book? You're really *weird*, Mom."

He retreated to his own room in disgust.

I hope he was wrong about who will read this book. I hope girls and women (as well as men) *will* read it.

The issues discussed here are those that revolve around the lives of what we usually think of as "the minister and his family." A man who is an ordained minister, married to a woman who isn't, with a couple of children as yet undecided.

This book (contrary to Andy's thinking), is aimed primarily at them, and especially at the wife in that marriage.

But some of the issues, I have discovered as I talked with other women about this book, do not just touch ministers and their wives. As I was working on chapter 5, which deals with the two-career marriage, I discovered that the problem of time, for example, concerns everyone who is struggling to cope with two demanding careers in one family, not just the minister's wife. The problems of who does the laundry and who takes Johnny to the dentist are with us all. In that sense, this book might be helpful to others.

I am aware, too, that the "typical minister's family" is rapidly changing. Lots of ministers are single, or female. They may be women married to men who are engineers. They may be men married to women who are also ministers. They may be women who are ministers (Presbyterian) married to men who are ministers (Methodist).

Nor is there any guarantee that both members of a ministerial marriage will be Christian. One might be an atheist, or a Buddhist.

But in order to write this book, I have avoided as many permutations as I could and tried to deal only with the pattern described above that still constitutes the vast majority of clergy marriages: one minister, one wife (both Christian), and—possibly—a few children.

There *are* two areas, though, in which I have stepped out of that pattern. In chapter 4, I deal with the former minister's wife, now divorced. In chapter 5, I briefly discuss the "clergy couple"—a term used for the sake of brevity when talking about two people, married to each other, who are both ministers. In both chapters, I discovered that the people concerned—having learned how to cope with the problems and opportunities peculiar to them—have an enormous amount to teach us all.

Stages

There are a number of assumptions underlying this book that need to be made clear at the beginning. The first one is that ministers' wives, like other people, go through the kinds of "stages" in their lives that Gail Sheehy, Roger Gould, Daniel Levinson, and others have documented in the last few years: operating on the model Erikson had fleshed out for children, and barely outlined for adults, they have proceeded to elaborate the plateaus, hills, and valleys in the adult's life cycle. The movement from one stage to another may be painful, but it is a "growing-up" experience:

> What I'm saying is, we must be willing to change chairs if we want to grow. There is no permanent compatibility between a chair and a person. And there is no one right chair. What is right at one stage may be restricting at another or too soft.

19

During the passage from one stage to another we will be between two chairs. Wobbling no doubt, but developing. If I've been convinced by one idea in the course of collecting all the life stories that inform this book, it is this: Times of crisis, of disruption or constructive change, are not only predictable, but desirable. They mean growth.[1]

I am not attempting in this book to make any statements about how ministers' wives, or anybody else, *ought* to approach their lives. Or even how to deal with the "stages" in them. Gould and Sheehy do that better than I can.

What I *have* done is described the changes in my own life as I felt myself moving through these stages: the same ways of "seeing the world" that were documented in *Passages* and *Transformations*.

What is peculiar about my story is that I am a minister's wife. So there are certain issues that color these changes/stages for me: issues like living in a parsonage; being married to a man who works peculiar hours; a man whose function as a priest gives him symbolic value far different than that of a teacher, say, or a movie director, or a plumber.

It is those issues—as well as the changes in my attitudes as I moved from one "stage" to another—that I will attempt to discuss in this book. That discussion may be helpful for other ministers' wives.

Choices

A second assumption I have made is that it is possible for each of us as human beings to make conscious choices. I have outlined several possible attitudes a minister's wife is able to take about her position. She can actively help her husband in his career, as a helpmate (chapter 1). Or she can choose to remain in the background, quietly keeping things calm on the home front so that he is free to exercise his ministry as fully as possible. That is being an enabler (chapter 2). She can declare herself free from either role and make her own way, as liberated as possible (chapter 3) from the preconceptions of the people she encounters. Or she may want to pursue her own career actively in the secular world (or as an employee of the church, ordained or otherwise). That is discussed in chapter 5.

For me, those various ways of seeing the world were progressive. I moved from one to another in a way that corresponded to the movement through adulthood that Sheehy and Gould describe.

That does not mean I am assuming other ministers' wives must go through the same progression.

That is important. I happened, for example, to bring a twenty-three-year-old's consciousness to the role of helpmate. Someone else who encounters that role at the age of forty might bring a completely different and much more mature consciousness to it. But the issues she will be facing might be similar, and the choices she will have to make might be the same.

What I am trying to say is that none of these positions is "good" or "bad" in itself. Each possesses enormous potential for growth *and* unrest *and* contentment.

Some women might find one position is a better fit than another. They might find that being an enabler, for example, is very much in tune with their personality, and they will do their growing within that framework, testing out other positions only to return to the enabler role.

In addition, no matter which attitude/stage/position we happen to choose, we may at times find ourselves under pressure from society to choose otherwise. Many women, for example, (not just ministers' wives) have described to me an enormous pressure from society to "do it all," almost as if there were *no* choice. Be a mother with perfect children. Have an immaculate house. Manage a career. Pick up a degree or two along the way, and above all, jog every day for a couple of miles.

This book will not tell you how to do that. It *will* stress that it is essential for each of us as minister's wives and as women to decide for ourselves how we will live out each phase of our lives. "Conscious" and "choice" are the key words. We are not, as women, defined either by our husband's occupations or by the expectations of the immediate society in which we find ourselves, whether that be a rural parish or an inner city church. We define ourselves.

Faith

A third assumption is that we do not do that defining without help. We are in God's hands. If we search within, the tools to make the choices will be provided.

A fourth and related assumption is that we are all members of the community of faith; and as such, we are *all* "ministers." Not just those husbands who happen to be ordained, or those women who have also taken ordination, are ministers. We are all—ordained and nonordained—equally participants in the essential ministry of the church, along with every other member of our congregation: "The basic ministry in the church is the ministry of Jesus Christ, and *anyone in the church*, whether ordained or not ordained, will be 'in ministry' only in so far as the ministry of the Christ is finding expression in what she/he is doing"[2] (italics mine).

These are implications I attempt to spell out in chapter 3. "Projection" and "shadow" are concepts it might be helpful to understand, so that we do not try to insist that our husbands—or ourselves, or our children—must be somehow more saintly, more generous, more *Christian* than other Christians. That is too heavy a burden to bear. None of us should be condemned to always having to be "better." Ministry belongs to us all.

Family

Another assumption I have made revolves around a statement a minister's wife once made to me. I have heard it echoed in different words by other wives—not just wives of ministers—since. "My husband," she said, "told me at the beginning of our marriage that his responsibility to the church came first, before me, before any children we might have. He loved me very deeply, he said, but our family would have of him what the church could spare."

I believe that the first priority of anyone, man or woman, in any occupation is his or her family. I understand that may be a difficult statement to make to someone who feels deeply the responsibility of one's calling. And I do not wish to denigrate the power of that call. But I think we Christians sometimes feel ourselves to be in sole charge of making God's presence felt on earth—we aren't. God is. And he is powerful enough to look after that. It is all right to be a father or a mother, a husband or a wife, sometimes. God is with us.

> One's commitment to an occupation . . . is always qualified and may be for a specified duration. One can change occupations without sin; one may not without sin abrogate one's responsibilities as husband or wife, father or mother. In any conflict between marriage and family commitments on the one hand, and occupational commitments on the other, one's basic responsibilities to marriage and the family must be understood as primary. Married clergy should seek to model this priority.[3]

That doesn't mean we disobey all other claims on our person. No one is free to be simply father or mother. The church as an employer *has* the right to make claims on us. But when the balance shifts too far in one direction or the other, it is our responsibility to stop, assess the situation, and try to bring it back to center.

Finally, I have attempted to write this book out of a thoughtful faith. What does it *mean,* in terms of our faith, to enable ministry to take place? What does it *mean,* in terms of our faith, to care for the woman who is turning to your husband in her loneliness?

The answers to those questions are highly individual. But perhaps this book can help minister's wives—and others—look at them closely.

I

The Helpmate

She needs to recognize that she has a choice: to be a little girl playing with toys, or to grow painfully into a woman who walks by the side of her husband . . .

Lila Miller

When I sat down to write this, I looked back carefully over thirteen years of marriage. I had changed. I was calmer. Without flinching I could watch my children in mad chase of panic-stricken gerbils on the loose in the living room. I could smile gently as all the pots and pans in the kitchen were pressed into service for the nine-year-old's series of complex scientific experiments.

Perhaps a new maturity was appearing.

The world had changed, too. The consciousness of an entire generation of women had taken a mighty shift outward. They had begun to demand new areas of equality and less static roles around the home. My own consciousness had shifted, too; several times.

I thought about my husband coping with these shifts. How often had he found himself married to a different woman than the one he had started out with?

Only last week I had been talking with some brand-new soon-to-be-released-on-the-pastorate ministers' wives. I recognized them easily. They were me, thirteen years before. "Once in a while," one confided, "I get a bit frightened at what's ahead. Sometimes it sounds pretty heavy."

It is. Maybe that is why people in congregations and ministers and ministers' wives themselves need to know that, like the people in Gail Sheehy's *Passages*, ministers' wives also go through "predictable crises"; and that these are not to be dismissed as mere difficulties to be lived through, but as valuable stages in development.

Every person is unique. The stages I outline—those of helpmate, enabler, liberated woman, career woman—are labeled as I happened to experience them. Another woman might experience them at a different time in her life, or in a different way; or might choose to emphasize one stage or another as the one she feels is most appropriate for her.

I've talked to enough minister's wives, however, who have recognized themselves in some of these stages, to believe that at some time, in some way, they affect us all.

The first stage in my life as a minister's wife I entered when I said "I do." But I wasn't able to identify it until recently, when I heard a young seminary student's wife speaking out of it. "We've been talking," she said, "about what we should do if someone's been in an accident, and your husband's away, and you're the one who has to tell the relatives."

"What an interesting assumption," I thought. "If the

husband's away, the wife will fill in. That wouldn't happen to a surgeon's wife, or an engineer's."

It was a familiar assumption, though, I remember. When my husband was ordained, I cheerfully gave up my teaching career and set out with him to our first mission field (note pronouns). So much for my career. I would spend my life assisting him in his. I would be—in what I now think of as my helpmate stage—his assistant, co-pastor, and lifetime vocational associate.

There is both beauty and pain associated with this approach. Both are important. The beauty of it lies in a kind of risk-taking that—in a career-oriented world—is becoming increasingly difficult to manage.

We managed. We packed up our wedding china and flew North. Eight hundred miles north of Montreal, to the edge of the world—the Quebec/Labrador border.

I still have my description of that land, the home I saw first from several thousand feet up: "It is a tortured country, glacier-worn, slashed red by the ore-hunters, populated infrequently with black spruce, coated with caribou moss. In one place, a forest fire burned uncontrolled. No one bothered about it. It seemed that only what was under the land was valuable, and the fire couldn't hurt that."[1]

The most astonishing aspect of all this to me, as I look back on that early retirement from my secure and well-paid job, is that I didn't think twice. I simply went—and fell illogically, instantly, and totally in love with a land most North Americans never see. "I remember that often we would get up at night, wakened by a blizzard, and watch the wind shifting the snow into mobile shapes, turning the innocuous school playground we faced into an Ungavan desert."[2]

27

We lost ourselves in the North; snatching leisure moments to fish or hike and to delight in this barren, half-ugly, half-magnificent country. Toronto, the city, my old job were a planet away.

Years later, when the teacher shortage was transformed all over North America to a teacher surplus, I would have a few moments of recrimination. "How," I would ask myself, "could I have dismissed so airily a job that is now impossible to return to?"

But later still—now—I am grateful I did. And what I have been aiming at, trying to say with these descriptions of the snow and the spruce, is this: *the risk was worth it!* It was more than worth it. The risk was essential to the blossoming of a part of me that would have always lain buried if I had continued in the safety of my Toronto classroom.

That is the beauty of this stage. There is something about following the person you love into an unknown future that is crucial to the human spirit. It bound us very tightly together.

A life, I discovered, that is defined simply in terms of "career" is too narrow. I understand now, looking back, the motivation of the hang-gliding enthusiast, or the parachutist. They are simply living out physically those times in our lives when we *must* jump into space, and leave familiar ground in order to be free. That is what we did. And I am glad.

Of course, there *were* problems. Oddly enough, they were linked with my own youthful energy, and the very commitment and love that had enabled me to go to the North. They represent the dark side of the "helpmate" attitude—the side that would eventually force me into another stage.

I was going to be the best minister's wife the world had ever seen. The house would be clean, the coffee on, and the Sunday school lessons prepared. My enthusiasm (and lack of understanding of my limits) knew no bounds.

The major problem with this was an inevitable submergence of my identity into that of my husband. Both of us became very deeply involved in the life of the church. Breakfast sounded more like a meeting of the church staff than the sleepy conversation of newlyweds.

There were crunchier issues in terms of day-to-day living, too: money and the manse.

The problem with the former was simple. There wasn't enough. We were facing the stark facts of life, a limited budget in an isolated northern community with an inflated (for those days) cost of living.

I remember quite clearly the day reality hit me. The initial excitement of our arrival had worn off, and we were skipping from paycheck to paycheck with nothing left over. And I wanted something, a dress or a parka, I forget which. I looked at my husband (sniffing, I think, with a few tears running over).

"Is this the way it's *always* going to be?" I asked (I was twenty-three).

"Yes," he said bravely (he wasn't much older), "that's how it is."

It looked like an awfully long life. My lovely dream of the elegant young hostess with the gracious smile began to fade. We both cried.

Furthermore, there was that other problem. The parsonage. It *was* extremely comfortable. We were rattling around in one of the few single-family dwellings in the small mining town. My plan was to spend my day floating easily through my chores, thus being available later to do whatever ecclesiastical tasks needed to be done. The only floating that really took place, though, was by articles in the basement when I let the wringer washer run over. It didn't empty properly. And one day in a fit of malice, it gobbled up my still-new honeymoon negligee and spit it out laced with grease and with pieces missing.

And there was no drier. Clothes were hung in the basement, and dried stiff and very wrinkled. I didn't want to ask the manse committee for one, either. They had already been very kind to us. Besides, I was used to paying for things by myself. It hurt to be dependent.

Both those latter issues need exploring further. This is as good a place as any, since it was at this point I first met these problems. They pop up again later, of course, in other stages.

Money

Lucille Lavender says in *They Cry Too* that "out of 432 occupations (listed by the U.S. Department of Labor) clergymen (in terms of salaries) ranked number 316. Clergywomen ranked 317, their salaries half that of their male counterparts. Clergy rank . . . with unskilled labour. . . . Though they rank next to the *bottom* economically, *educationally* they rank with the top ten earning occupations—lawyers, physicians, dentists, [etc.]"[3] (italics mine).

William Presnell, a United Methodist pastor and Director of the Tenafly Pastoral Counseling Center in New Jersey, pinpoints the problem neatly. It is not so much that there isn't enough (although sometimes there is not). It is that clergymen are not sure how much they have a right to ask for. He noted a "passivity that is the plague of ministers" and an "ambivalence clergy couples feel about speaking up for adequate support."

> The couples in this study seem on the whole reluctant to negotiate openly for increases in salary and benefits, especially when they are serving churches where such professional negotiation is not common in the work life of parishioners. . . . When they perceive themselves as servants a maintenance wage appears to be a natural feature of ascetic discipline. When they consider themselves as professionals, a wage comparable to that of other professionals . . . seems more appropriate.[4]

That is the exact center of the money issue for clergymen. Are they dedicated servants or competent professionals? They often can't decide. And, as Presnell says, "this results in a certain amount of guilt and anger."[5]

Guilt: "How can I dream of asking for more money when two miles from our house is a group of native people living in deplorable conditions?" And anger: "But after all those expensive years at the university, I'm earning less than my neighbor who finished school at grade ten!"

Presnell sees the issue as a matter for the couple, even though it is the minister who is the servant/professional. And rightly so. The whole family—unless the wife is working, which is an issue to be discussed in chapter 5—is dependent on that income. As Robert Kemper, consulting editor for *The Christian Ministry*, points out, "Poverty is a virtue, but it is virtuous when linked with chastity. We have a long and honored tradition of married clergy, of clergy with families. What is virtuous about raising a family in an affluent culture on subsistence wages?"[6]

The resolution to the guilt/anger syndrome Presnell mentions does not lie in discreetly leaving the room when

31

the question of one's salary comes up (some clergymen do that still). It does lie in finding a healthy balance between servanthood and professionalism, asceticism and materialism; between "freedom from obsessional efforts to 'be good' on the one hand and from the bondage of libertine life on the other."[7]

The salary issue is simply part of the entire ascetic ideal—the ancient emphasis on purity, withdrawal from the world, and obedience—an ideal that has been too rigidly interpreted. We need to look at it again. Most of all, we need to relax. It is all right to have fun. Lots of Christian doctors, plumbers, and business people do. It doesn't make them any less spiritual.

We *have* gone a long way toward changing that ideal. Women no longer sit dourly in church, shrouded under large hats. Ministers dance, cry, and wear blue jeans. Their children are no longer conceived by osmosis; the stern art of self-denial is no longer practiced in terms of sex or laughter. Perhaps it is time to stop practicing it in terms of salaries, too. In addition, a too-rigid interpretation of what clergy "ought" to earn is bad for one's self-esteem!

> Clergy do not think they are worth very much. They harbor notions that those in other vocations know more or do better work than they themselves do. I think that is nonsense. In an increasingly specialized world, the generalist is becoming the most valuable member. Persons who cross generational lines, meet personal and communal needs, counsel and teach and communicate are extremely valuable. If there were no clergy at all and if these services had to be purchased on the open market, society would pay enormous fees for what clergy do on modest salaries.[8]

Once we shift away from "a too-legalistic interpretation of the ascetic ideal"[9] the whole subject of the minister's remuneration becomes part of a different series of questions. First, how much money is he/she entitled to as a professional in today's world? Then, just as important, how does he consciously make thoughtful use of it? How do he and his family use their financial gifts in the light of their Christian values?

Those are sticky questions. They place emphasis on the minister's own stewardship. As individuals and as couples they must do their own wrestling, and make their own choices, rather than simply having choices made for them.

Those choices may involve tithing, or a heavy investment in education for one or all family members. They may mean travel, a holiday, swimming lessons. They should be choices arrived at by a conscious reaching down into one's own self and values, rather than simply assimilating values provided for one by either the institutional church or society; this is not easy. And it is all too easy to rush headlong into the values of a society that measures a human being's worth by the size of his paycheck.

One needs a healthy sense of balance. Presnell sees an attempt toward that kind of balance taking place.

> Clergy families are rebelling against the harshness and legalistic interpretation of this ideal, while still recognizing it as a valuable guide to spiritual discipline . . . replacing unquestioned obedience to the vow of poverty, stewardship increasingly becomes, after honest assessment of one's own needs, *an act of conscious self-giving of that which one might have chosen to withhold.*[10] (Italics mine)

That rescues the clergy couple from the kind of empty self-righteousness that comes from having choices made

33

for them. I detect that quality in myself from time to time. It's a faint internal "hrumph" I make whenever someone I know takes off for a holiday in the sun or buys something I covet.

There is an inner demon that is saying, "How unnecessarily extravagant. I would never be so un-Christian as that." Of course I would. I am, whenever I have a chance. And who is to decide whether or not it's "good" or "bad" or "Christian"? Certainly not I. One must decide for oneself.

In the end then, it is important to speak up for a fair salary, instead of grumbling internally or suffering needless worry from paycheck to paycheck. Manfred Holck, Jr., the editor of *Church and Clergy Finance*, recommends exploring with the church board such items as: base salary, salary increases, pensions, housing allowance or parsonage, Social Security, health, disability and life insurance, vacations (and a day off a week), continuing education, professional expenses, and car allowance.[11]

Arthur Bell, president of Ministers Life Resources, writes: "First, I suggest you find out the salaries of the local public school junior and senior high school principals. The educational qualifications for your job and theirs are similar; often the hours are similar; the visibility of the job may be comparable."[12]

It is a painful, difficult, hurting issue. Your local church may not want to face it. You as a couple may not want to face it. But the issue is not going to go away. For us, it popped up later when we had children. (Johnny's needing a new snowsuit every year or two certainly makes you look at the salary issue.) And if one finds oneself in a two-career marriage, it will pop up again. ("She's working, so perhaps we can help the squeeze on the church budget by not giving him much of an increase this year.")

On our first pastorate we would have been wiser (after carefully assessing our needs) simply to have asked for more money, but we did not. We were too proud. I went back to work instead.

That turned out to have two benefits. One, it solved our immediate financial problems. Two, and far more important, it was a beginning to the psychological work I needed to do at that point. I badly needed to discover that I did not have to live out my life as my husband's associate, submerging my career—and a lot of my financial independence—in his. It was the proper psychological work of the twenty-three-year-old.

Dr. Roger Gould, from his considerable research at U.C.L.A. into adult life cycles, suggests that people between the ages of twenty-two and twenty-eight share a common false assumption that "those in a special relationship to us can do for us what we haven't been able to do for ourselves."[13] That was my assumption.

I had been trying to piggyback on my husband's career, living out my ambitions through him. It would not have been especially healthy for either of us. I had to do my career work by myself. At this point I had no children, so I was perfectly free to do that.

I ended up teaching an assortment of Cree and white children: the first Naskapi Indians to have much contact with the white man, and the children of the engineers and miners in the town in which we lived.

I loved it. I slowly developed ways to approach the problems of two cultures in one classroom. I reveled in my new competence. And my husband reveled in his new wife. We did not have to talk about the church all the time.

It came to me rather belatedly that what he did not need was a vocational associate. What he did need was the separate human being he had married in the first place.

Manse

I discovered that, just as with the money issue, there were ambiguities revolving around church-owned and maintained housing that manifested themselves in an absurd mixture of gratitude, love, and irritation.

I was grateful, on one hand, for the caring people showed toward us. It is deeply touching to move into a spotless house, beds lovingly made up, and fridge filled with casseroles and apple pies. But I badly wanted new curtains, and I didn't want to ask for them.

I was grateful that we—as occupants of church-owned housing—didn't have to pay the fuel bills (it is cold in northern Quebec). But I was having my first nudges of worry about equity. No one owned his own house there, of course. But what about later? That investment in housing is usually the biggest investment a family makes—and it is an important one during times of inflation.

There are, as I discovered later when talking to other minister's wives, other problems. One of them is the depth at which the parsonage is embedded in the collective psyche of a congregation. Sometimes the members feel their ownership of that house quite deeply. "The manse," Robert Rankin suggests in an article in *Pastoral Psychology*, "stands as a symbol of the pastor/people relationship."[14]

As such a symbol the house the minister lives in can make a lot of statements. At its worst, a manse can symbolize a "we own you" kind of attitude on the part of a congregation. "You are our minister and wife, and we will take care of you. In return you will be on call whenever we need you."

In the same vein, a comfortable manse, owned by the church, and furnished and decorated by members of the church can "create misunderstandings as to how much privacy the minister's family can demand."[15] Not that the misunderstandings are always on the side of the congregation. The congregations I have encountered have been remarkably discreet. But I found my own sense of obligation, mingled with my desire to be loving and caring, sometimes landed me in an entertainment schedule that was more than my family—or I—could cope with.

At its best, a parsonage can say, simply: "We care for you. Here is a comfortable place to live. We are glad you are here, and we recognize that this is *your* home."

There is one final and central ambiguity about manses that overshadows the others. It is this: as long as the board of stewards is there to replace the shingles if there is a windstorm, as long as the mortgage payments are never due, as long as the plumbing bill will never come to us, we will never become fully independent. There is a sense in which we cannot grow up, no matter how mature we might become in other areas.

That is a curious kind of protection, from a bittersweet goal. Gould, for example, describes his first foray into home ownership as one of the growth steps into his adult life. An immature part of himself needed to be sacrificed so he could take that step.

What died was a protective illusion connecting us to childhood and our parents. We could no longer believe that we were children on loan to California, destined to return to our "real" home. Only after the illusion died did we recognize its silent presence. In the back of our minds, we were protecting ourselves against the full realization that this was really *our* life, to be lived into an unknown future. A tether to our parents was torn, and we mourned it.[16]

The church—as long as it owns and maintains the manse—is a substitute parent, protecting us from the final reality that the sewer might someday plug up, and we will have to fix it.

That is not a good protection. It is better, for most of us, to negotiate for a housing allowance (or better still, simply an adequate salary) and provide our own housing, and accept the responsibilities that go with that.

That kind of protection explains why, to this day, I have such trouble approaching a manse committee to ask for things. "I need new drapes for the living room" sounds suspiciously like "Could I have the car tonight, Dad?" or "I need some money for a new dress." It places me squarely back in adolescence, with all the rebellious feelings that are a necessary part of that stage—but inconvenient in this one.

It also explains why my reaction to the idea that someone else might choose those drapes for me is inclined to be volcanic; no matter how lovingly they might choose, no matter how expensive and well thought out their choice might be. We all went through having choices made for us in childhood. We are too old for that now. But those childish feelings remain nicely intact within us, ready to explode when certain key words are uttered, such as "Wouldn't green go well with that carpet?"

I would like to decide for myself, thanks. And that is hard to do when someone else is paying.

The vulnerability inherent in that kind of anger means, ironically, that there *are* some valuable insights available to those of us who live in parsonages. We—the "ministers," the ones to "help"—then know how it feels to be "helped."

There is a sense in which ministry—our ministry to others—creates debts, debts of the spirit, that cannot be paid back, that are created out of love. They produce feelings similar to the ones I have when someone helps me wallpaper the kitchen, or retiles the bathroom for me.

They are grace-filled gifts. I need to learn how to accept them and maintain my dignity, and not keep trying to "pay back." As ministers—and I am speaking here of all of us, not just those who happen to be ordained—we also need to know how it feels to be ministered to, helped.

It is how Indians feel, and children, and people in the hospital, and people struggling with nervous breakdowns, and the dying—all of us, at some time.

Perhaps that is the use that can come out of the manse experience. If we *must* live in one, if we must forego, for a time at least, the maturity that comes with hammering on our own shingles with our own hands, we can perhaps attain the kind of maturity that understands giving and receiving with dignity. Grace. The kind of giving God does, no paying back, no loss of dignity, just love.

In the end, the two issues of money and the manse come together. Both of them circle around Presnell's idea that the ascetic ideal, with its sense of isolation and apartness from the world, is outdated. In the case of money, it is important to make decisions about how to use one's income consciously', as an act of service—by choice.

In a manse, too, it is better to give by choice. The hospitality of the parsonage means more if it genuinely comes from the love of the inhabitants for the congregation they belong to; a *conscious* giving of self, rather than an accommodation to a role.

To that end, then, one can try to make living in the parsonage as independent—as grown-up—as possible. Patricia Clarke (formerly associate editor of *The United Church Observer*) recommended the following to congregations after writing to assorted minister's wives:

> —Give her a small allowance. . . . It means she doesn't have to telephone the committee every time she needs a new clothesline, or she can buy curtains when they are on sale instead of waiting for approval and paying more.
> —Let her have a freer hand in decorating. Most wives are sick to death of insipid beige and institutional green.
> —Furnish the minister's home the way you like your own. [Better still, give them a furniture allowance and let them choose their own.]
> —Help the family feel the manse is *their* home. Don't inspect without an appointment.
> —Keep up the maintenance.[17]

You, as the minister and wife, can negotiate those things as you move in, or at any time. Some congregations are even setting up a landlord/tenant agreement with their ministers, to relieve some of the fuzziness about who does what around the property.

In any case, it is good to be as free from the people-in-the-parsonage role as possible. Then one is able to choose to be hospitable. Truly hospitable.

Reflections

What did all this mean? Though I did not know it at the time, the beginning of my first pregnancy was to move me into another stage. Not completely, though. One area of my personhood had come alive while I was busy being helpmate. I was not going to leave it behind.

For one thing, I had learned a deeper meaning of the word "trust." We had a brand-new marriage, untested in many ways. It took an enormous leap of faith to leave my job and jump into the unknown with this new husband, trusting that we would somehow look after each other.

That leap was invaluable. We learned that our relationship was solid enough to withstand my misguided attempts to drown in it. We also discovered that I was strong enough not to disappear completely.

The most important learning, though, was this: there is enormous female satisfaction in developing skills that match those of the man you love. My husband was—is—a good counselor and compassionate minister. I began to assimilate those qualities into myself, at the same time that he was learning he didn't have to carry the entire burden of our life together on his shoulders.

It was a good time. I have not forgotten it. In a large part of our life together, I am a helpmate still, but one who, as Lila Miller suggests at the beginning of this chapter, walks side by side with—not behind—her husband.

II

The Enabler

The miracle of being in love is too overwhelming an experience ever to be dismissed as a projection. I do not believe for one moment that a projection can in itself light up the whole world. It is the love which goes with it that lights the world.

—Irene Claremont de Castillejo

When you're down and troubled and you need some love
  and care
And nothin', nothin' is going right
Close your eyes and think of me and soon I will be there
To brighten up even your darkest night.

—Carole King

Just as I was coming to terms with the role of helpmate my life took another turn. I happily became pregnant. And my husband went back to seminary near Philadelphia. That was where I first consciously encountered an alternative to the helpmate role.

It was at a "theowives" (as the wives of the students were called) group. My identity secure in my growing belly (no longer just minister's wife or teacher, I was now also *mother*). I was listening to a new ordinand's wife talk about their first charge. "My job," she was saying, "is not to help my husband at his job. My job is to keep things running smoothly at home so that he is *enabled* to do the best job he can."

She went on to describe how she had organized her life—down to the box of Pampers in the family camper—so that whenever he was ready to take some time off, she was ready to go too.

That sounded pretty good to me. It took the load off my shoulders of constantly thinking of ways to help. And it affirmed the traditional role of wife and mother I was now very anxious to fit into.

I worked away at the idea. Our apartment, now that I no longer worked outside the home, became uncharacteristically neat, except for the teddy bears sleeping in the armchair, and soon, the fresh toothmarks on the hastily assembled Salvation Army furniture.

Our lives even became somewhat organized. Our second child was on the way (right on schedule) when we moved back to the parish, and I settled down to raising children and vegetables, in that order.

It was a rich and satisfying time. My husband seemed happy with the arrangement (although all this enabling enabled him to put an astonishing amount of energy into church work, more perhaps than was healthy). Our children painted in the kitchen and made mudpies and foxholes in the garden. And I studied and grew in ways that would have been impossible if I had still been pursuing my career. "One of the advantages of the traditional marriage is the very fact that the wife is not working for a living. Therefore she can develop and champion the broader and deeper aspects of life, and oppose the narrow and lethal definition of life as work."[1]

I found myself developing inwardly even as my children and vegetables were thriving. A very feminine, nurturing principle was at work. I was content. Except for one or two issues, which I am going to deal with in this chapter: hospitality—the listening ear and bubbling coffeepot instinct that is a part of that feminine principle, and a related issue, transference—or what can happen when one's minister husband listens kindly to a lonely woman.

They are powerful issues.

Hospitality

For me, hospitality meant the door was open, a fire was on, and I was welcoming to whoever needed a quiet visit. I liked that. There is something about having children, learning to hear what little people are saying when they don't have words to use, that makes one sensitive to all those times when any person wants to talk, but can't find the right words. It is a mother's skill that is so unrecognized by the world that it frequently dries up when the children are older, without ever having been recognized for the remarkable achievement it is.

"A child's chaotic and disorderly passions," says Gould, "require a woman who chooses a domestic career to become expert in the intuitive, phenomenological world, if she is to produce a viable and mentally healthy human being."[2]

I liked using that expertise. But it also aroused in me a certain ambivalence. I needed to be nurturing. But I needed solitude as well to do the thinking and dreaming that is also a crucial part of this stage. And the children—as they progressed into relatively comprehensible speech—needed time with me to use that speech, time to talk when Mom was not occupied with omnipresent company.

The balance between those two opposites was difficult to find, increasingly difficult, as we became more and more settled, and knew more and more people who felt more and more comfortable about accepting my breezy (and foolhardy) invitations to "drop in sometime. We live right beside the church."

Finally, as pressure increased, I went to work on it while I was away at a dream seminar. "How do I see my way clear to have some private time?" I asked myself one night. "Do I shut the door firmly and lock myself in my study (coming out occasionally to play with the children). Or what?"

The answer came that night with unusual clarity. First I had a complicated dream about a new birth. Then, "Don't try to paint a change in me," a disembodied voice suddenly declared. "I'm a *woman*. This is my business."

Being caring and nurturing—a "woman's business" in the best sense—seemed to be in order. I digested that. What, then, did I do with my need for solitude?

I was reading a new book by Henri Nouwen when I began to find an answer. True hospitality, he says, grows out of solitude. The two are not opposed. One is rooted in the other.

In solitude we can pay attention to our inner self. This has nothing to do with egocentrism or unhealthy introspection because, in the words of Rilke, "What is going on in your innermost being is worthy of your whole love." In solitude we can become present to ourselves. . . . There we also become present to others by reaching out to them, not greedy for attention or affection but offering our own selves to build a community of love. *Solitude does not pull us away from our fellow human beings, but instead makes real fellowship possible.*"[3] (Italics mine)

It had to be both/and. Not just being ever ready with the coffeepot, and not just the silence.

I had to learn to proportion those elements myself, too. No one else could tell me how much private time was necessary to sustain my times of involvement with others.

Like any other woman—especially any woman who lives in a house as visible as a parsonage—I had to choose for myself where the open door policy began and ended. And I had to *interpret* to others this need to do my home-work—whether it was raising bees, flowers, or children—in order to receive them freely and gladly.

I do know now that when the balance shifts too much to the "open house" side, I begin to feel sick: too much coffee, too much sitting, too much being still, and I start to fidget and wish that the visitor would go.

But when the balance falls too far in the other direction, it is worse. I begin to feel isolated and empty, and hungry both to care and be cared for. Most of all, I miss the sense of otherness, the pulling-out-of-self that occurs when someone is talking about the things that are important in his life. It is a deep human need, I believe, to live in and through someone else, to be with him or her in the sense that is all *being* and no *doing,* reaching out, in Nouwen's words, "beyond the limits of human togetherness to a new communion."[4]

There are ways to manage to have both hospitality and solitude. I discovered that I can set limits on the time I am "at home." I unashamedly do not answer the door or the phone at certain times during the day. (When the preschoolers are sleeping is a good time. Otherwise they will answer the door for you.)

Perhaps that smacks of "office hours." But I am starting to recognize that you do not have to be constantly available; as long as there are reasonably predictable times when you are.

I am trying to be active rather than passive in relationships, too. Instead of jumping when the phone rings, I phone first. I suggest a time to go skiing with the children, or shopping for Christmas presents, a time that suits us both. It is better than letting the phone dictate how I will spend my day, and just taking my quiet time out of the leftovers.

None of this is applicable only to life in the parsonage, of course. All women face these conflicts, especially when their children are little and in need of constant care.

But pressures are intensified for manse-dwellers. They simply know more people, because of the ministerial ability to thread through all strata of society. The opportunities for relationships are rich and varied, and so are the groups who might be invited to come. The women's groups, the choir . . . you do not *have* to invite them anymore, not in most churches. But you *do* usually have to make the decision as to whether you will invite them or not. That choice does not so often confront other men's wives.

It is easy to be ambivalent. I might feel too tired, for example, to have the youth group. But when we have had them in, they have kept me young and have been a priceless troop of older brothers and sisters for my children.

Or I might not feel like having the visiting missionary from China. "The budget," I would point out, "is suffering from too many meals."

"Can't we just have some chili?" my husband would ask, blissfully ignorant of the rising price of hamburger. So I would throw together another batch of chili, muttering grievances under my breath, only to feel my anger transformed to warmth by the careful attention the visitor is paying to the advancing pregnancy of the six-year-old's guinea pig or his discussion about Peking Duck with the eight-year-old.

Nouwen describes the redeeming quality in these encounters.

> While visiting the University of Notre Dame . . . I met an older experienced professor who had spent most of his life there. And while we strolled over the beautiful campus, he said with a certain melancholy in his voice, "You know . . . my whole life I have been complaining that my work was constantly interrupted, until I discovered that my interruptions were my work."
>
> . . . What if our interruptions are in fact our opportunities, if they are challenges to an inner response *by which growth takes place*?[5] (Italics mine)

It works out. Somehow, it is possible to learn to juggle the time alone and the interruption times and the time together. That was the proper learning for me to be doing at that time. The broadening and deepening that was going on as I struggled to balance the conflicting demands of my role and my own personhood was valuable for our marriage and our children as well as for me.

> If the only life valued as meaningful for men or women is a work life, then the hazards of both the traditional and the two-career marriage are increased. If a meaningful life is defined as one *centered around deep human contact, then the hazards of both life styles are minimized.* And in a culture where deep human contact is valued, then parenting a child is not idiot's work, but one of the most difficult, challenging, demanding and important tasks in life.[6] (Italics mine)

Transference

Of course, there were still hazards. That brings me to a discussion of the other issue of this time. Let me tell you about Fran.

She blew in one evening after a meeting we had both attended, cigarette package in one hand, one skinny knee protruding from a hole in her blue jeans.

Not in good shape was Fran. She had four children, a run-down townhouse, and a habit of not eating.

We spent a lot of time talking. I couldn't resist that temptation to play big sister. Besides, she was so unconventional, beautiful in her weightlessness, with her huge dark eyes and lovely cheekbones, and tousled black hair.

Fran came to the house more and more often. Soon almost every evening would find the door swinging open, or the thin face appearing through the hole in the hedge, come to join us for after-dinner coffee.

When her husband couldn't find her, he would phone me. If she wasn't with us, I would know where she was.

Soon her dress began to change. The jeans were tidier; more like my own. Soon she was attending some heady night courses, like me. A weekend camp for children I was helping with found Fran there too.

I was flattered. She was struggling so hard to change. She used my recipes. She even planted a garden in imitation of my annual summer obsession.

Ah, Fran. It still hurts to think about it. My pride in the unconventional friend that even I—the minister's wife—could have. The ego satisfaction of having someone wanting to be so much like me. Wanting—I began to suspect as she talked to my husband—wanting to *be* me.

Until finally the relationship began to cool.

Fran, I noticed, appeared with annoying frequency just when I was putting the children to bed when I wanted to spend time with them.

Or she needed desperately to have something picked up, and could I get it as she didn't have the car to get to that particular store?

Or she would have unexpected company and would need to borrow something from my freezer.

Then the crises began because (I concluded later) Fran still needed the relationship. But as I began to send mixed signals ("Yes, you're welcome here" with a smile that was only a little forced) the only basis on which she could come was with a legitimate crisis.

Then we (Jim and I) would have to be with her. That was our role, after all, as the-people-who-lived-in-the-manse. So her children were sick, or someone would have a lump here or there, or the always shaky marriage would sway dangerously.

And on and on. Until finally I realized (belatedly) that I was out of my depth, at the same time that Fran's marriage *did* finally break up, and she fastened her affections elsewhere and left town, to appear infrequently, and finally not at all.

Poor Fran. And poor me, left with my sense of failure in a relationship, and my guilty suspicion that I had been both used and a user. She was lonely and struggling. Most of all, she was strongly attracted to my husband. She made me sharply aware of a word I had heard mentioned in our house, especially when my husband had been doing his clinical training, "transference." I made haste to find out what it meant.

For one thing, it is the "Problem Clergymen Don't Talk About" according to Charles Rassieur in his book of that name. It is the problem of the lonely woman, badly needing to be cared for, who is therefore prone to falling immediately, overwhelmingly, and quite unintentionally in love with the first strong male figure in her life who *does* care. Her pastor.

This is not an easy situation for the pastor. It is even less easy for the pastor's wife. As one angry minister's spouse put it:

> The problem is that like other men in a personal helping profession, such as doctors, counsellors, or teachers, our men have a sexual appeal to women, tied to their roles and professional function. This situation is often flattering to the men . . . the thing that makes the situation so sticky for wives of ministers is that we—as part of the church community—have to hang in there being cheerful and loving.
> . . . There *are* women who manipulate for affection and approval. We are left with little else to do but hang around and smile pleasantly. Do you understand what I am saying? The psychiatrist's wife is seldom put in a position of socializing and being loving toward the unhappy housewife who is desperately in love with her husband.

That is what one form of transference is all about. John Ordway, Director, Division of Mental Health, Municipal Court Psychiatric Clinic in Cincinnati, enlarges the definition. "The term 'transference' means that feelings, impressions, in fact human reactions of any kind are 'transferred' from one object *or situation* to another. . . . A

51

person makes contact with a new situation or person, and, in addition to seeing present reality in the latter, *brings old impressions to the new contact*"[7] (italics mine).

To oversimplify, a woman brings all the need for tenderness, love, and nurturing she may have experienced in her childhood—or may now need in her marriage—and plops it squarely on her pastor. She falls hard, because, as James Davison points out, "The pastor is a perfect set-up for transference, especially as a father figure, both in the pulpit and in counseling."[8]

If he is not prepared to handle that (and, Davison cautions, most ministers don't have the kind of training that will allow them to use transference in its deepest sense) then the situation is potentially awkward.

"Counter-transference" (again, to oversimplify) is the term used to describe the phenomenon in which the feelings of the pastor become fastened on this flatteringly admiring parishioner. His response (as Ordway describes it), may be "as if the good fairy had finally showed up; and they enthusiastically embrace the opportunity in a blaze of passion AND idealism. The word 'idealism' is used because it is by the unrealistic IDEAL image of womanhood that the clergyman is affected hotly and strongly."[9]

The situation does not often go that far. Nathaniel Lehrman rightly points out that a loving sexual relationship in the minister's own home is a great buffer. "Hence," he says, "the great importance correctly placed, I believe, on the happiness of the minister's home life by Protestant and Jewish churches and temples."[10]

That is important. However, lest we feel we can do nothing in this situation but greet our husbands at the door each evening in a filmy negligee (à la Marabel Morgan), let us look at other ways of dealing with the issue.

Dealing with Transference Situations

The first way to deal with transference might be for both the minister and his wife to take advantage of whatever training is available to them in this area. Or, if only the husband is able to take clinical education, it is helpful if he can explain very fully to his wife all the learnings he has about this dynamic: preferably before they find themselves caught up in it.

Marriage Enrichment weekends, with their emphasis on developing strong lines of communication between husband and wife, would be helpful.

> Wayne Oates has observed that "the Protestant pastor functions as a counselor within the context of his identity as a married man." A marriage affirming each partner's freedom and responsibility will be a positive resource for the pastor as he copes with the occurrence of his sexual attraction to the counsellee.
>
> If a pastor's marriage is preeminently a dialogical relationship, there can be appropriate opportunities for a pastor to share with his wife the kinds of feelings he has toward a counsellee. If husband and wife are open to each other's being, and if they affirm each other's freedom to be, the basic framework will exist for them to face the issue of heterosexual feelings each of them has toward other persons.[11]

Those open lines of communication are important. That may sound trite, but it is true. My own husband indicates that part of the reason we have avoided counter-transference problems so far is his sure and certain knowledge that all such feelings can be shared with me, his wife. (That *does not* mean he is sharing someone else's secrets with me, just his own feelings.)

I can share my feelings with him as well. Let us not kid ourselves. A minister's wife is not exempt from falling in love, or being attracted to another person, or even having someone else fall in love with her. Being aware of that, and accepting the beauty that is in it, may make one more understanding of the woman who is attracted to one's own husband. We are less likely to denigrate those feelings in another person if we are in touch with them in ourselves. Virginia Rassieur writes in her own chapter in her husband's book:

> The awareness of my own sexual response to men is a continuous unfolding. . . . Some women surely know this about themselves already. Others may have more difficulty acknowledging a sexual response to men other than their spouses, but I believe it is there within each woman. To become aware at this level we must put aside the early teachings of our culture: that "nice" girls are not sexy; that they do not try to affirm their sexual selves. Getting right down to it, this denial and avoidance of my own sexual response has led me to a confusion of feelings in the past. My buried feelings struggling to make themselves known startled me and clouded my effort to make responsible decisions about my behavior. I found that probing for awareness undercuts the need to flirt and introduces the opportunity *to contemplate how to act appropriately.*[12] (Italics mine)

Somehow an awareness that responsible behavior in such a situation is both possible and necessary takes away the feelings of guilt ("nice girls—especially minister's wives—don't *feel* this way") our culture endows us with. One is *not* condemned to translate feelings into physical actions. One *is* allowed to luxuriate in the fact that one is both lovable and capable of loving; and gloriously sexual to boot.

That understanding then makes it possible to care for the lonely woman who sees your husband as the answer to her prayers. It is possible to be hospitable in Nouwen's sense, in the sense of being present to another in a deep way. She is hurting, alone, and probably bewildered. If one is well armored with a healthy marriage, it may be possible to listen, visit, maybe walk with someone who needs nurturing. That is fulfilling. It is also good therapy to spread the dependency so that she is not simply involved with one person—her pastor. Helping her form relationships with other people—in the church, maybe—can be part of that nurturing.

Allowing her into your caring at a point in her life where she is vulnerable may help her see the reality of the situation: her minister is not unattached. He is part of a loving home and church community.

None of this is suggesting that it is not possible simply to get help from an outside consultant if the situation gets out of hand. Your own right to solitude is crucial. And none of this is easy. Sometimes it is better if the minister simply refers an especially vulnerable counselee to someone more experienced. Again, there are no "shoulds" here, only choices.

Like the issue of hospitality that this is part of, it is a double-edged sword. Somehow, we have to walk the middle of it; nurturing and allowing independence, being with another, and retaining time for oneself.

Those are narrow lines to walk. But we need to walk them if we are to grow. These are problems of love, of the heart of the human condition. "We come no farther in our understanding by . . . denigrating [the experience] as [simply] 'transference,' "[13] James Hillman, former Director of Studies at the Jung Institute in Zurich, wisely says.

Connected with that problem of love is the need to pray. I am not saying that lightly. This question of love/transference is best dealt with when one is in touch with one's innermost self.

> Indeed, I may love to the uttermost outwardly, but should the vertical connection to the ground of being within myself, to my love of myself, toward myself, by myself, not yet be formed, I will have stirred up a love that cannot please . . . To be in touch with you I need to be in touch within.[14]

Finally, transference, as Ordway points out, can take many forms. Some experts go so far as to say transference is a factor in one form or another in all human relationships. It is not always loving; sometimes we transfer deep feelings of anger; and it is not always sexual. But the experience is nearly always valuable, if we allow ourselves to learn from it. Let me tell you about another friend of mine.

I met him in my creative writing class, the one I teach in a nursing home. He is old—although not as old as many of the residents. He is only seventy-two. But he is completely crippled. He can move only his head and one hand, very slightly.

He is not book-educated. "Got as far as grade three," he admits cheerfully.

All day he sits in his wheelchair. At six o'clock every evening he is lifted into bed, where he stays until someone lifts him out the next day. He is ugly, swollen with fluid from his enforced idleness.

He is proud. He is determinedly cheerful, despite the

fact that he is in constant pain. "Hemorrhoids," he tells me abashedly.

He tells wonderful stories, which I tape and then transcribe for the book we are writing in our class. He is an old friend of my father's. And I love him dearly.

Clearly, it is a case of transference. I am aware that part of my feeling for him is transferred from—connected with—the love I have for my father.

That does not make my affection for him any less miraculous. Nor any less valuable to us both. For how (I reason to myself) can I learn to love the broken, crippled, weak parts of myself if I cannot learn to love this broken old man?

Perhaps that seems a long way from the lonely woman in your husband's office. But I think that is where the root of both the problem and the solution lies—within ourselves. We deal with all these feelings from as much knowledge as we can muster, as much training as we can get, and as much love and caring as we have available.

Reflections

What did all this enabling and loving mean, finally? My children were growing older. There were fewer mudpies in the garden, and more schoolbooks thrown through the door at the end of the day.

This had been a time of immense contentment. There is something deeply satisfying for a woman in living out the traditional, very feminine values of her culture: gardening, cooking for her family, discovering the maternal side of her nature, and allowing its fullest expression in relationships with her children and with other people.

But part of me was getting restless. I began to have recurring dreams of skiing, diving off cliffs, taking bold risks. Gould says that people in their thirties experience a new kind of opening up. I had been happy living my life roughly according to the pattern my own family had set down for me. Mother raises the children and provides warmth in the home. There were wildflowers on the table in summer, and in winter I stripped paint off old furniture and sanded it and waxed it till it glowed.

But it was time to move on.

> Her only real task is to resolve her internal prohibition . . .
> then she can work without feeling abandoned, or forced out
> there; or she can tap some of the satisfaction inherent in a
> domestic career. Many women . . . come to understand they
> are not breaking any rules by making a life for themselves,
> and therefore they happily begin a career in their early
> thirties. In the mid to late thirties, this issue takes on even
> greater urgency.[15]

I had done my home-work, then. Not that it was ever to go away. I had developed an important side of my nature. I was never going to let that reflective nurturing side go. As a woman—not just as a minister's wife—I know that I cannot avoid the role of "carer." I have to accept that it is as much a part of my femininity as having breasts and a soprano voice.

The risks are high. I could be accused of arrogance. I risk again the disillusionment and guilt that came with Fran. But minister's wife or not, amateur or not, all that I am as a woman says that all healing does not take place in the therapist's office; that creative listening is not the sole prerogative of the pastoral counselor. My own forays into being truly hospitable to another person—man or woman—can help me understand the woman who reaches out to my husband and all that he symbolizes. And I am strong enough and wise enough and caring enough to cope with that.

III

The Liberated Woman

It's funny how often they say to me, "Jane?"
"Have you been a *good* girl?"
"Have you been a *good* girl?"
And then when they have said it, they say it again,
"Have you been a *good* girl?"
"Have you been a *good* girl?"

A. A. Milne

Meanwhile life was ticking on. The children were growing older. Jim was still working hard, and I was continuing to study. "Synchronicity" was one of my new words. In Jung's writings, it refers to a coincidence with meaning—when fate seems to step in and take a hand. Fate stepped in and produced a new pastor's wife in our area. She brought a new consciousness to the prayer group we ministers' wives had been having. We talked a lot.

"Some days, I feel as if my husband has a mistress. Always the church comes first," someone said.

I perked up. The bride-of-Christ as mistress. What an

interesting thought. The church did take up a lot of time and devotion, I had to admit.

Someone else said: "I really need quiet time, to think and recharge my batteries. Even if the house gets messy."

And someone else said: "Well, sometimes it's my husband's turn to clean up. And by the way, how come we have to keep providing luncheons for those meetings of theirs?"

Enter a new word. "Enabling" began to slip out of my vocabulary. "Liberation" was coming in. I emerged from my teacups and confronted my husband, who is—fortunately—a wise and understanding man.

"I think," I said bluntly, "we've got enough tomatoes for you to make chili for the team meeting tomorrow. And by the way, why *don't* you go on that hiking trip next weekend? I'd be glad to preach for you."

At that point, I wasn't sure what internal myth I was living out, or why it was so important for me to leap from my kitchen to the pulpit. But I knew this wasn't simply a regression to stage one. I was not doing this simply to help my husband, nor was it in any spirit of enabling. I was doing it for me. I had something to give that involved words, and I needed the opportunity to focus on an idea, to ground it in my faith, and use it to lead the people in worship.

I was terrified.

But Jim went hiking, and I sat down and put the service together. It was a giant step in releasing me from the fixed patterns I had become pleasantly enmeshed in. As Gould points out, it was time to move on. "Opening up to what's inside" is the way he refers to the work of any person at this stage. Jung calls it the work of the second half of life—developing the deepest parts of the inner person. I was off on a voyage of discovery. "What we begin to encounter in the late twenties and early thirties are the interests, parts of ourselves and values that we will develop during the remainder of our lives."[1] I did not know that. All I knew was that I needed time to do the sort of thing my husband had been doing: preaching, leading in worship. I needed to get in touch with the masculine side of myself, Jung would say. I needed to be able to work alongside my husband as a competent individual.

And it was no coincidence, I realized later, that I wanted to be competent *in his field*. Again, I was working on some of the issues that had been with me in chapter 1. Jung says we fall in love with those people who fulfill the unrealized parts of ourselves. I was on my way to growing up some more—no longer realizing ambitions through him, but through myself.

I am not alone in this. Very often I meet ministers' wives who describe a pull to enter the ordained ministry themselves . . . perhaps as a way of legitimizing much of the work they are already doing, but also as a way of recognizing the deep urge they also have toward spiritual leadership.

All of this led to dealing with the expectations of the congregation as to what kind of minister's wife they now had. And that leads to a discussion of the twin phenomena of projection and shadow. They are useful terms for the minister's wife.

Projection

Esther Harding's definition in *The "I" and the "Not-I"* might be a good place to start.

The term projection, as used in analytical psychology, refers not to something that you have thrown on another but rather to *that factor in yourself, of which you were entirely unconscious,* that has been caught by something in the object and so made visible. Your psychic content becomes available to you because it has been mirrored in him.[2]

It is as if we carried a reel of film around with us all day on which was portrayed in miniature all our qualities, both good and bad; but the only way we could see these qualities was to use someone else—a friend, say, or husband, or child—as a screen on which these attributes could be projected. Then they are completely visible. Unfortunately, we never realize they belong to us; we assume them to be attributes of the other, when he or she is simply acting as a screen on which to receive them.

This is further complicated by the fact that we tend to project our unknown attributes onto someone who *does* possess the quality (kindness, for example, or vindictiveness, to use a dark quality) to some slight degree. That "hooks" the projection so that we (the *unconscious* we) can sustain it. Everybody does this.

It is common knowledge that we project qualities upon other people and dislike, or positively hate, the other person for some characteristic which we unconsciously share ourselves. So long as we only see black shadows on someone else, we can take no responsibility for them in ourselves. We merely hate the other fellow. . . . The bright shadow qualities, on the other hand, of which we are unaware, we envy in other people. I doubt if we ever envy qualities which do not intrinsically belong to us.[3]

My dreams usually try to warn me when I am suffering from a particularly bad case of projection by portraying me standing in line at the movies, or sitting in a movie theater,

63

with the sound of the projector whirring away behind me. Then I know I need to start looking inward.

> A good way of learning to detect one's shadow is to notice what qualities in others make us angry or irritated. [Note: Castillejo here is talking only about the dark shadow.] We should allow ourselves to feel angry or irritated with other people to the full. And then when we have calmed down, if we turn our thoughts inward and enquire whether we have some similar quality in our own nature, on some level or another, we can generally find it. If we can succeed in doing so, the projections we had made on the other person will be automatically withdrawn because it is only qualities of which we are *un*conscious that we project.[4]

It is helpful—especially for the minister's wife—to become aware of what she might be projecting onto other people. And, just as important, what *they* might be projecting onto her husband, and onto her. The nature of their role as a couple could mean that they might receive some interesting projections.

All of us know in some way that our priest/husbands have certain virtues attributed to them simply because of their jobs.

> The congregation may want to project on him the parts of themselves they value as important, so he will feel powerful, admired and probably effective. . . . His only proper response may be to endure this projection without being led into pretentiousness and vanity about himself, so that the congregation seeing his lack of regard for their manipulation . . . will be assisted to renew their search for the conception of God.[5]

That kind of projection does not happen to a plumber or an architect, although it does happen to some extent with doctors.

David Switzer puts it beautifully. "Every professional who has clients is not only who he is but also who the other person feels him to be, and the source of much of the strength of those feelings is part of the person's unconscious processes. We are not only persons, but symbols.[6]

The symbolic dimension—for the minister and his spouse—is extremely important. Because, underneath the congregation's conscious awareness of who he is, there is the sure understanding that the man who wears the flowing robes on Sunday is "a physical representation of the whole community of faith, of the tradition, of a way of viewing the meaning of life, of the dynamic power of faith, *and of God himself*"[7] (italics mine).

I have a friend who would insist when we were all convulsed with laughter at a party on a Saturday night that she was going to wink at Jim when he came up the aisle the next morning. "Then he'll remember and he'll laugh," she would chortle, "just when he's supposed to be *very solemn.*"

But on Sunday in church she would lean over to me and would whisper, "I can't do it! He's turned into *a minister!*"

The clergyman, at a totally unconscious and very primitive level in the minds of the congregation, represents no less than God the Father.

That gives him unique and very healing power when it comes to being with those who are sick or in crisis.

Our bringing our bodies to a bedside . . . does present the person and the family with what may be for them a powerful symbol, and this may in itself elicit some response, activating deep resources of strength in the form of feelings of safety or security, the diminishing of anxiety, a sense of peace.[8]

But that dynamic also affects the minister's wife. If he—at a deeply unconscious level—is symbolic of God, that makes his wife—at the same level—Mrs. God!

It is important to be aware of that. I believe the lack of awareness of just what is being projected upon her by individual members of the congregation can be a source of real frustration for a minister's wife. She can become caught in a conflicting web of expectations or become completely mired in a slough of attempts to be what everyone thinks or suspects or imagines she should be.

The power in this kind of symbolism cannot be underestimated, especially in an age of rationalism like our own. People become hungry for pegs on which to hang meanings, ways to organize the material of the spirit. When the "spirit and meaning stuff" is not given a place of honor in society, it develops an energy of its own.

Those projections onto the pastor's wife take various forms. One, for example, might be of a certain amount of saintliness. Everyone *consciously* knows, for example, that a minister's wife is as cheerfully sinful as the rest of humankind. But again at that *unconscious* level, she may be believed to be always gracious, somewhat asexual, and never less than totally loving. Mrs. God is always put-together.

One expectation that I have particular difficulty with is frugality. The ascetic ideal I mentioned in chapter 1 is still alive and well in my psyche.

One time my husband and I wanted to go on a trip to Antigua. Some friends were going, and invited us along. We were tired, and it was winter, and we had some money left in savings from my teaching days. "Why not?" we said to each other, growing more and more excited. Why not, indeed . . . except for one small voice inside me that muttered, "But what will people *think*—such extravagance!" I squelched the voice. It was a struggle. But the beach was wonderful. I need to squelch that voice more often.

I had rightly realized that if anyone expected me to be always gracious, or always thrifty, that was their problem (actually, fewer did than I thought). The real danger does not lie in the presuppositions people might have about us. Those are unconscious, and as such, innocent. The *real* danger is that we will absorb those projections and suppositions and expectations and try to be saintly, kind, frugal, and generous all the time. Then their problems become ours, in spades.

The human psyche has a way of compensating when the "good" side gets out of control. The minister's wife who tries always to be perfect at the expense of her own feelings will have the shadow side of her personality slip out, willy-nilly. Perhaps she will be sweet all morning teaching Sunday school and then come home and have a fight with her husband over lunch or kick the dog or scream at the children.

The Shadow

The dark side has to come out. The shadow. Esther Harding describes its operation.

> There is the "I," the ego, that represents what I call *myself*; then there is the *persona*, the mask that I wear to show to the world; and there is still another part that I know, or partly know, exists, but which I prefer to keep hidden because it is unacceptable to the world—this is called the *shadow*, and it is usually almost entirely forgotten—that is, it becomes unconscious to myself, although it may be quite obvious to others.

67

> When the "I," the ego, comes into being and becomes the
> focus for consciousness, it is as if a light were lighted in the
> room of the psyche that had formerly been completely dark.
> As the light is small, it illuminates only a small part of the
> room. The rest is in shadow; its contents are invisible. But
> they are not nonexistent.[9]

So the minister's wife who tries valiantly to "carry" all
the expectations she perceives around her, who is unable
to deflect unrealistic ideas of what she is or can do, may
develop an enormous "shadow" side, which by definition
she is unaware of.

A Minister's Life and Casualty Union pamphlet entitled
"Despite Appearances, Ministers' Wives Are Only
Human" pictures on its cover the grinning papier-mâché
mask of a haloed woman. It is a graphic depiction of what
can happen psychologically to an unwary woman. She
might get caught in a Halloween face, and the "real" her,
both bright and dark, cannot emerge, and repressed, will
take on enormous energy. The Minister's Life pamphlet
suggests what happens to some ministers' wives.

> We may not feel obligated to be in church every Sunday, but
> most of us feel the wife of our pastor must always be in the
> front pew. Where we can watch her.
>   And of course, we also expect she will always be
> appropriately dressed (by our standards), keep a perfectly
> neat home and raise a brood of ideal children—all on an
> extremely modest budget.[10]

If the minister's wife is at all successful in living up to
this somewhat exaggerated portrait, she may become the
type of person Harding describes as appearing to have no
shadow. She is perfect.

> We see this sometimes in a group where there is someone
> who is "completely right," who never, never raises his
> voice, never says an unkind thing about anybody. [S]he

seems to have no shadow, no natural human weakness. But then his [her] shadow falls on the other members of the group, and they are compelled to express his [her] negative and all-too-human reactions. They find themselves making critical remarks that are really more incisive and destructive than would be warranted by their own feelings. For there is something peculiarly exasperating about someone who has no shadow. We find ourselves obliged to disagree with him whether we want to or not.[11]

That can have unfortunate results for her friendships. And it may lead her to have some interesting dreams, as the shadow attempts to bring itself to her attention. In one of mine, I was with Jackie Kennedy Onassis. We were going to a choir practice in New York, in one of the poorer sections. She was going to lead the practice. We drove most of the way in her car, which was a discreet purple, matching her dress.

That dream says nothing at all about what Mrs. Onassis is like. It says a great deal about how I perceive her from the press. And it says even more about my own shadow. Like her (as the press portrays her, at any rate) there are parts of me that want to be the queen bee and lead the practice; to be royalty (hence the purple).

Such a dream is demanding that I be honest with myself and notice that such a queen-bee quality is within me, as well as the desire for power and wealth. No use denying it. The demands clearly are present, and I must talk to them. Above all, they are not to be buried deeper. Then they can really get out of control.

James Hillman, the former director of studies at the Jung Institute in Zurich, suggests the problem of these shadowy sides of ourselves is really one of self-love.

The cure of the shadow is a problem of love. How far can our love extend to the broken and ruined parts of ourselves, the

69

disgusting and perverse? How much charity and compassion have we for our own weakness and sickness? How far can we build an inner society on the principle of love, allowing a place for everyone? . . . If we approach ourselves to cure those fixed intractable congenital weaknesses of stubbornness and blindness, of meanness and cruelty, of sham and pomp, we come up against the need for a new way of being altogether, in which the ego must serve and listen to and cooperate with a host of shadowy unpleasant figures and discover an ability to love even the least of these traits.

Loving oneself is no easy matter just because it means loving all of oneself, *including the shadow* where one is inferior and socially so unacceptable.

Loving that shadow may begin with carrying it, but even that is not enough. At one moment something else must break through, that laughing insight at the paradox of one's own folly which is also everyman's.[12] (Italics mine)

Of course. Perhaps that is why dreams are so funny. I laugh at the suggestion that part of me is Jackie Onassis, even as I am shaken by her presence. "Hello," I must say. "I see that you are there, that part of myself that loves sleek clothes and money and is proud. I will not try to pretend that you do not exist."

Cure [is] a paradox requiring two incommensurables: the moral recognition of those parts of me that are burdensome and intolerable and must change, and the loving laughing acceptance which takes them just as they are, joyfully, forever. One both tries hard and lets go, both judges harshly and joins gladly.[13]

A friend of mine—also a minister's wife—was describing to me a house she wanted to buy, the house that is out of reach. "The worst thing about it was my feeling of shock," she said. "I thought I had accepted the fact that I would not have my own house, that I would always live in a parsonage. But I hadn't. I want this house so badly. I am obsessed with it." We are only human, she and I. We are not above wanting.

Sometimes if a friend gets a new fur coat or a new house, I am envious. But I no longer struggle to push the envy away. It is part of my shadow. I own that feeling, and I must talk to it. "Yes," I say to myself gently, "you want a new coat too. Well, that's human. That's all right."

Part of the problem is that "bright shadow," the "Mrs. God" projection that some members of a congregation might unconsciously wish you to be. What do you do about those people who wish you to be good for their sakes? They may be refusing to live up to their own potential and are asking you to carry it for them.

> If we do not live up to our own potential, the positive qualities will be repressed into the shadow, and we will have what I have sometimes called a bright shadow instead of a dark one. When we project this bright shadow onto someone else, the person who carried the projection will seem to us to be "always right," able to do easily and well the things that are difficult for us, and so on. We burden him [her] with our expectations of his [her] abilities instead of acquiring for ourselves the possibilities of achievement which are potentially present in us. A person who is content to take an inferior position, who prefers to have an easy job rather than to buckle down and develop himself and his work, and who then admires and overadmires someone else who does things well has projected his bright shadow onto his neighbor.[14]

There is not much you can do if you are part of a congregation that has a large number of people who wish to live out their virtue through you. That is their problem, just as your unlived shadow is yours. Their growth to wholeness, their getting in touch with their shadow is part of what they are doing by belonging to a church community. Their business as members of a church is becoming whole. Their shadow is *their* business, and God's.

However, it is possible to reflect back their shadows for them by refusing to pretend if the projections do not fit. Then those virtues (or vices, for that matter) belong to them again. Chapter 1, for example, described the struggle ministers and their wives often have with their image as dedicated servants versus competent professionals. How do you negotiate a reasonable salary if you and your congregation perceive a ministerial couple as two people who are content to live on less than others do?

Negotiating for a salary commensurate with his skills is one way a minister can break that projection, and ease his wife of the "fine thrifty woman" projection some minister's wives must carry. Of course—and this is important—the image may be the reality. Many ministerial couples *do* wish to live extremely simply, and are able to present to their parishioners an alternate life-style that springs out of the core of their being. In that case, they have chosen. They are not carrying an expectation placed upon them, and they *are* free in a very real sense.

All this does not mean that one suddenly starts snarling around the church, bent on redressing the wrongs of centuries. Nor—to continue the example of negotiation above—does it mean suddenly demanding an immediate large raise. That would be tactless and hurtful. It does mean that we need not be afraid to be human. To let the warts, bumps, freckles, and lumps show. Masks are for Halloween.

Another practical help is a support group. A weekly meeting, say, of the other ministers' wives in the area, can provide a forum for "allowing" the bumps and freckles in an atmosphere that is accepting, where one's fellow participants won't be shocked. You can practice on each other. Other ministers' wives are not perfect either; but some of them may have valuable insights to share.

Projection and the Minister's Family

There are further complications. A child I know used to come home from Sunday school and tell his parents in tones of horror that "God's little boy was bad today."

People project things onto the minister's children, too. It takes courage to withstand the conviction that one's own child—the minister's child—will be better somehow than everyone else's. Again, the risk is of an unknown and uncontrolled parental shadow. He or she might even end up having to live out the shadow of the adults in the house, if they have been unable to come to grips with their own.

> The compulsion to live another's shadow is most apt to occur within a family relationship, where the interaction of the members of the group is so profoundly influenced by unconscious factors. It can be the cause of neurosis or of delinquent behavior in the children of parents who have refused to accept the responsibility for their own shadows: the children have to live the shadow side.[15]

Philip Marchand describes the problem of the child as scapegoat familiar to family therapists.

> This technique of scapegoating is so familiar now to family therapists that it no longer causes much surprise. It is almost a bad joke. In fact the first premise of a family therapist is that the "problem child" is almost never the real problem of the family. She or he is usually the most vulnerable and sensitive member of a family (almost always a child), who becomes

the "problem," a scapegoat for all the hidden conflicts within the family system.[16]

Beware therefore, the ministerial couple who is perfect. The children may have to inherit their darkness.

Finally, it is important for both minister and spouse to be aware of the symbolic function of the minister even within the family. The minister's wife is even more aware than anyone else that this shepherd of souls may need to be cared for in his own weakness. But she is also as affected as anyone else by the enormous symbolism of his priestly function—unconsciously. It is difficult to have an argument with God. It may be hard to remind your minister/husband that it is his turn to take out the garbage—especially if he is getting ready for the several hundred people who wait to hear his every word on Sunday. That makes garbage detail or dishwashing pale in comparison.

Perhaps the answer here lies in learning to be angry with God. We have been taught for a long time to believe that God the Father, in his infinite wisdom, will look after all things. He is strong enough to do that. That means that he is also strong enough to take your anger. As a matter of fact, any relationship benefits from anger being released instead of being bottled up, especially one that is as important as one's relationship with God.

And that may mean that the time one spends on prayer is infinitely important—not just in terms of one's own being, but also in terms of the marriage. Practicing telling God what you think of him sometimes makes it easier to confront the priest/husband with his apparent lack of concern, say, about the state of disrepair of the children's bicycles. Of course, God might point out an irrational tendency on the part of the minister's wife to presume—with others—that somehow her minister/husband should be more perfect than other husbands. Not only should he not forget to fix the bicycles, but they should be done yesterday. *God* is on his side, isn't He?

The minister is human. Recognition of his humanness makes life a little easier for the minister's children, too, especially when they are adolescents. It is difficult for any teen-ager to make the break from home and find his/her own feet. "At 16, 17, or 18," Gould says, "our work *to take on some of our parents' power*, to become independent of their world view, is painful and traumatic"[17] (italics mine).

When our parents' power is somehow all wrapped up with the power of God, that may make the leave-taking infinitely more difficult.

> I never had a decent, much less an indecent, adolescent rebellion. As the elder son I took on the family mantle, accepted the expectations laid upon me, particularly by my father, and sought to be a success as a Christian and as a minister.
> . . . For the first forty years of my life I obeyed the prescription given to me: "Get good grades, work hard, be a leader, succeed. . . . No rebellion. I was the son who stayed home. The son who would have to leave home in middle age.[18]

It took Robert Raines many years to work out that "leaving" that he had been unable to do as a young man—the separation from his bishop father.

> Part of my inside said, "You're right, Dad." Another part of me said, "Bullshit, Dad!" I had displeased my father in the process of holding onto my own integrity. I did not then know whether I was also displeasing my father God. . . .
> I entered into a period of several years of struggle with my

75

father in which each of us, now standing on separate turf, sought to understand himself and the other in new terms. The Bishop and the son of the Bishop!"[19]

Of course, no one *thinks* of her husband or father as "God," or even as his associate (although I remember our then-two-year-old, eldest son regarding his father benignly over dinner one night: "How was God today, Dad?" he inquired, much as one might politely ask after the health of one's best friend's mother). All of this is not carried on in the realm of "thinking" any more than the adolescent's urge to rebel is a thought-filled gesture or the elderly lady's assumption that you would be charmed to head up the bazaar is a conscious act. It all goes on in some other realm than the rational, and as such it has great, primitive power.

The task of liberation is to bring that prehistoric dynamic up to consciousness, simply to become aware of it, bubbling away in us as efficiently as in everyone else. And then to relax, to be oneself, not to absorb the virtues and vices thrust upon one, not to project them onto anyone else. That is freedom and liberation.

Reflections

What did it all mean? This sudden demand to have my husband take on some of the feminine tasks, while I went to work on the preaching?

It meant first of all that part of the work of this period was coming to fruition. I was learning, as Gould suggests is necessary in one's early thirties, that the statement "there are no significant contradictory forces within me" is a "major false assumption."[20]

Of course there are contradictory forces. I had buried them nicely in stage two in order to be free to work on the important issues of that time: developing my own powers to be hospitable and loving.

Now other forces were rising. In my attempts to come to grips with—and disentangle myself from—the projections people place upon people-in-the-manse I found myself face to face with the problem of my shadow. The "significant contradictory force." The dark unknown part of myself I hadn't wished to look at. My own ambition.

I had been plagued with recurring dreams of a shark; an ancient, dark, ruthless beast, devouring everything in its path. In one, for example, I dreamed I was swimming in a lake. I thought I felt a shark graze my leg. We all got out, somewhat unbelievingly. But when we climbed up and looked down into the clear water, we saw the shark floating there, looking big and dark . . . I dreamed about a house with water running through it, so we could all swim when we wanted to. Except a tiger shark gets in and then we can't swim at all. We wonder if it could even be a great white. When I forced myself to look closer at the beast, I recognized him. He was my own hungry need to be heard, to have a voice, to be recognized as an equal.

He had to be answered, even—as Hillman suggests— even loved. So I began to take services, work at workshops and seminars, develop a new competence outside the family.

And I began to accept that I was not always nice. I was human, sometimes tired, often cranky and manipulative. I set out, finally, to own my own shadow:

> Strangely enough, when we take up the shadow side of our own personality, renouncing the silent claim to be entirely

white, immaculately moral, the effect we produce on our environment undergoes an unexpected change. For, when we carry the burden of our own human weakness consciously, other people are relieved of it. As long as we remain unconscious, we cast a shadow dense in proportion to our conscious rectitude; but when we carry the shadow consciously, its blight no longer falls on others, and we begin to give the impression of being more complete."[21]

One minister's wife whose marriage, strained for years, finally broke down, was astonished at the way people stopped wanting her to be perfect. "People started swearing in front of me again," she said, in tones of wonder. "I hadn't realized how dehumanizing it is to be always treated as special."

That is what liberation is. It is the ability to insist on being human, bruises and all, to resist stereotypes—not just from others but from oneself. It is the work Jesus did when he greeted the woman at the well as an equal and forgave the adulterous woman. It is the kind of loving forgiveness that we owe to the undiscovered parts of ourselves.

IV

Divorce and the Minister's Wife

"But I really want a marriage in which the two of us are together because we make it better for each of us separately. I want a marriage in which I can keep on growing without worry that I'm moving away from my husband. I want my own life and our life. I want to believe that it's possible," she said fervently, and then leaned back and asked, "What do you think? Is it possible?"

—Recorded by Ellen Goodman

This chapter is different from the others in this book. Like the partners in 79 percent of American marriages, I have never been divorced, nor am I considering doing so.

That is one difference. The other difference is that I have learned more from this chapter. That is important, and it underlines everything I would like to say in this part of the book. Former ministers' wives have a great deal to teach us all, single or married, male or female, about the roles of minister and wife, about the church's role in relating to single people, about loss, guilt, and grace—and about surviving.

The first thing I learned is that clergymen and their wives do split up, with alarming frequency. "The dangerous practice of becoming all things to all people, and conforming to roles that are not real, can all have a devastating effect on marriage. So much so that *among professionals, clergymen rank third in the number of divorces granted each year.*"[1] They are not alone in that splitting up, of course. "One out of every twelve women age 35-54 is currently divorced (it is now one of ten for women who have had at least one year of graduate school beyond the bachelor's degree) and one out of every eight is either widowed or divorced. Most of them will not remarry."[2]

The reasons for divorce are as complex as the reasons people have for marrying in the first place. Some causes stand out, though. Ellen Goodman isolates one major factor. "Every divorce," she says, "is a story of change."

> People don't always develop in the same direction . . . How many divorced people have we heard say, "We grew away from each other. . . . We didn't have anything in common anymore . . . We both changed . . . He seemed like a stranger. . . . I couldn't talk to her anymore. . . . We are just different."
>
> As complicated as it is for one person to change, it may be geometrically more complicated for a relationship to change.[3]

Another reason lies, not with the couple themselves, but with the society in which they live. It used to be that men and women had to obey strict role patterns (man—provider, defender, *and* ruler; woman—nurturer of the old, ill, and children) in order to survive. As

Douglas points out, the role for ministers' wives was a strict one.

> . . . the author concludes that her goal should be [in 1832] "the advancement of her husband's ministry, the salvation of the souls committed to her pastoral charge, and the alleviation of their temporal wants. Let her feel on becoming a clergyman's wife, she had as it were, wedded herself to her husband's parish, and to the best interests of his flock."[4]

But that changed.

> Factories, transportation, schools, hospitals, and modern merchandising changed all that. Man and woman no longer need marriage in order to survive, and marriage has ceased to be basically practical and productive, but has become instead a special kind of friendship. When it fails to provide us with companionship, sex, and the satisfaction of our individual emotional needs, we are deeply dissatisfied—no matter how many goods and services the spouse provides. . . .
> Ultimately responsible [for increasing divorce rates] is our expectation that marriage will be an emotionally satisfying relationship.[5]

People—and society—are changing. Sometimes the marriage cannot keep up, and it collapses. What does all this mean in terms of clergy marriages?

When I talked to several former ministers' wives, they made it clear that clergy marriages are subject to the same dynamics as everybody else's. One partner may outgrow the other. They may have been immature at the beginning, and eventually grew up different.

Few of them blamed the breakdown of their marriages on the church. "Our marriage broke down because of other factors than the church. . . . In fact, we stayed together longer because of the fact we were in the church.

The death of the marriage was a fact that had taken place long before we split up."*

Stress Factors in Ministry

They did point out, though, that there were factors in the vocation of ministry that can create enormous pressure on a couple. This can make problems within the relationship more difficult to resolve: even though the relationship might have reached a rocky point anyway, sometimes the strains inherent in their roles can simply tip it over.

Take the personality issue, for example. It is not the "church's fault" if clergymen are different from other men. But, according to Rabbi Jack Bloom, writing in *The Journal of Religion and Health,* as a group they *are* different—distinctly so.

> One might then hypothesize that the men who become religious professionals, who enter a world of differentness and otherness, do so because of some strong personality determinants that may differentiate them from the rest of the population. If this is so, if this is not a myth, then there is something *different about these men*.[6] (Italics mine)

When Bloom explored the hypothesis, he came up with an assortment of traits.

> Both Stern *et al.*, and Siegelman and Peck found that theologians tended to be somewhat more openly succorant and nurturant towards others. In addition they tended to be more dependent on them for affection.[7]

*Unacknowledged quotations in this chapter are from conversations with several ex-wives of pastors whose names are withheld, and are marked with asterisks.

Kagan says that a man who has been denied sufficient love and attention in his childhood may choose to become a clergyman "because in that role he is required to give love and attention generously to other people. Acting out his own childhood frustrations, he *sometimes overdoes his attention to his congregation.*"[8] (Italics mine)

This is not to say that all ministers had an unhappy childhood and have overwhelming needs to be accepted, liked, and respected. But—according to Bloom—it is an observable pattern. And for those who act it out unthinkingly, it can place enormous strains on their marriage.

I think there is a certain kind of person who enters ministry. They are always rescuing people. Even when I needed help, when I was having babies, my husband was always rescuing someone else.

Then they don't have the time to spend with their families. Being busy and rescuing people means you don't have to be part of the marriage relationship.*

Not being part of the marriage relationship may be part of what Bloom describes as a quality of isolation, of being set-apart from others, which, perversely, may lead them into an over-involvement with others.

That one may resolve one's set-apartness by "merging or over-involvement with others" seems strange, but it is plausible. It is also indicated by some of the research that has uncovered personality similarities between ministers and, of all people, research or physical scientists. . . . Dittes, pointing to research done by Bier and Schroeder, noted that both clergymen and scientists show a kind of "observer and commentator role in society which protects them from getting fully involved in active participation in life."[9]

83

All of these attributes are neither good nor bad in themselves, but it is important to be conscious of the dynamic. It is, again, the issue of the shadow discussed in chapter 3. If there is a hungry child within, it is better to know and love that child than to let him remain in darkness and be pushed into a constant struggle to have-everyone-love-him-all-the-time. If there is a cool observer in a white coat as part of one's psyche, better to know him, so the observer can be saluted as important, instead of being half-drowned in a flood of good intentions for all.

It is important to have one's eyes looking inward as well as out, so one can *choose* the basis for action. "I wasn't blaming the church for our divorce. People *choose* the way they're going to spend their time. Including ministers."

The responsibility for easing a load of workaholism— according to that former minister's wife—rests with the workaholic.

All the blame for being overworked cannot be laid at the door of the minister, though. Like the "friends" of the alcoholic who ply him with martinis, the congregation of the workaholic minister often *does* expect him to be on constant call (like God). And the pattern of the minister's work week is such that on Monday (the day he might relax before his week begins its acceleration toward Sunday) most people are refreshed from their weekend off, gearing up . . . and phoning the minister with suggestions about meetings and projects.

Many people in a typical congregation also have totally unrealistic ideas about what their minister does with his working day. Seeing only what he does for an hour on Sunday, they presume that the rest of his week is dedicated to that hour. Even if they *are* active in the weekly activities of the church, they may not realize that frequently he has commitments he must honor at other levels of the church than the local one.

So he is saddled with the task of interpreting his job to the very people he serves. He may simply be too rushed—or unaware—to do that.

There are other factors besides a common ministerial profile and congregational expectations that add to the stresses of a couple within the church who are having problems with their relationship. One separated minister's wife, considering reunion, told me how difficult it was to go back to the parsonage. "We would have the whole congregation chittering about it. If a lawyer's wife wants to go back, then she can, and try again. But how *could* I go back now? I'd be the 'bad girl coming home,' which I'm not. There is such a sheer lack of privacy."

The need for a pastor is sometimes expressed, too. "So many ministers have the idea counseling is for someone else," one woman said. "Because they are counselors themselves, and they seem to need to be so strong."

So, a failure in relationship takes place. Not because of the church; but sometimes aggravated by the stresses inherent in being an employee of the church.

What then? What happens to the minister's wife who finds herself no longer a minister's wife?

According to the people I talked with, she then has all the regular run-of-the-mill problems everyone else has, and then some. She has some special gifts, too. That helps.

Special Problems of the Ex-minister's Wife

What are the problems?

The first one is a sudden loss of community, especially

if the woman's life has been very bound up in the church. Helpmate type people, for example, are the most vulnerable to this and to a related loss of identity.

> When we left our pastoral charge [on being divorced], he went to his new church, to a furnished manse. I gather his new congregation was very good to him, supporting him, inviting him for dinner, even doing his laundry sometimes. His new presbytery was there to help him. His conference personnel officer called on him.
> I found myself in Montreal with nothing. No furniture. No dishes. No money.[10]

(That furnished parsonage again. It rears its head at every stage of marriage. Or un-marriage.)

About her attempts to join the fellowship hour after service in her new church she says, "All around me I could see people drinking their coffee, and having animated conversations. But only with their friends. The good church people literally parted around me, like the Red Sea around Moses."[11]

Another former minister's wife says that the older people from her congregation found the breakup most difficult to handle. "One day in the supermarket I ran into a woman we knew well. She smiled broadly, happy to see me. Then suddenly she remembered. Her jaw dropped, and her face went still. The whole thing was just impossible for her to accept."

It is hard to know why this happens. One divorcee wonders if the well-known practice of setting the minister and his wife up as an example of all that is good and admirable isn't to blame. When the minister's marriage fails, it causes ripples in other potentially shaky marriages in the congregation.

Another mentioned that "the people who seemed to

have the most trouble with the breakup were those who were having problems in their own marriages." The illusion of health they had been projecting onto the ministerial couple had been destroyed.

Related to the loss of community is a loss of identity. This is especially true for a woman whose life has been bound up in the minister's-wife role. If she has cheerfully swallowed all the projections of the congregation (and her own expectations), she may find herself both separated and remarkably empty when the marriage is over. "My personality was based on the man I was married to," says Vidal S. Clay, a twice-widowed and once-divorced lecturer in family relations at Connecticut University, "and when he left me my selfhood foundered."[12]

Living in a furnished manse may mean there is no equity to divide at the end of a marriage. Living on a small salary may mean there is little in the way of savings to divide.

When we married, congregations preferred a minister's wife to devote her extra energies to church work—and that was where my talents and my interests were. But just like Iris Murdoch, for my thirty years of work, I end up with nothing. When my husband retires, I won't even share in the pension I helped him build up.[13]

Guilt—a factor for many women in a divorce—hits ministers' wives particularly hard. "I found it difficult to go to church. I would cry all through the service, and then not be able to go back to that church again. It was really a feeling of guilt over being part of a marriage that had failed. *It was strongest when I went to church.*"

Of course. It is the Protestant churches that have particularly stressed the ideal of the family as one to reach for. It is there that the former minister's wife will most feel

87

that she has somehow let down the people who mattered. Or maybe even God.

Gifts of the Faith

Tom York is a divorced minister. One is confronted at the breakdown of a marriage, he says, with a "sense of massive failure." But that leads us directly to the gifts inherent in the whole situation for the former minister's wife. She is usually a Christian. And—like the faith of Tom York—her faith may undergo a remarkable expansion.

> That there is a future, and that it is in God's hands, is a Christian belief. I know that I now relate to a tenet of faith that never before had meaning for me—Christ's second coming. Previously, this aspect of Christianity seemed to be something that fundamentalist preachers and the desperately poor harped on. Now I too hunger and thirst after Righteousness and strain forward (for who can go backward?) towards Love's second coming, for the reign of Truth, for Peace on earth, and for a little unfamiliar Mercy in life.[14]

> One of the things you need to remember is that you are still a child of God. No matter what has happened, He won't let you go. That feeling grew in me. And I was able to let the past go.*

Some former minister's wives describe how—although the church as a congregation had a terrible struggle relating to them—*individuals* at every level of their denomination (not just local, but at the national level as well) did not seem to share in the bewilderment of the structure and ministered to them with great compassion. " 'Would you like a church?' the personnel officer said to me. 'I'm sure I can get you one (a position as a lay supply).

I know you can handle it beautifully.' He was willing to go out on a limb for me. I really needed to hear that. To know that he thought I was competent."

As church people, they were willing both to listen, be available, and to learn; which leads me back to the point I made at the beginning of the chapter. As Christians we have a great deal to learn from the divorced minister's wife.

The Need for Rituals

First of all, we need rituals to accompany divorce. The church plays a large part in the movements of life: birth, marriage, and death. In the death of a marriage, it is at a loss.

This only reflects the confusion all of society feels:

> I can remember exactly when I became aware of the differences between the two experiences, death and divorce. Stephen, the children's stepfather, had walked out of the house in anger the night before. He had not returned. Now at dinner time the children and I were standing around the kitchen while I was cooking. We were uneasy, unhappy. No one said anything, but each of us knew that we were alone again without a father. Robbie spoke up: "Mom," he said, "where are the neighbors bringing in food?"[15]

We know what to do when a person dies. We do not know what to do when a marriage dies.

It may be that we—as a church—have to lead the way in showing people how to *be with* people who are mourning. By somehow refusing to recognize and approve the need to mourn a divorce, we are implicitly stating the marriages are not *supposed* to end, that someone is at fault, that we will turn our collective ecclesiastical back on this error, and perhaps it will go away.

This only ladles more guilt onto the heads of those who already have more than their share. "You of all people" (one woman was told), "to be divorced. You're the *woman*. It was up to you to keep the marriage together!"

Penelope Washbourne suggests that our role may be simply to be present, to share, in a sense, at the death vigil, to assist the divorced person to do her grieving and despairing:

> The only way to emerge strengthened from despair is to go into it.
>
> . . . A woman whose life seems destroyed by the end of a marriage and whose basic sense of herself is radically shaken cannot pass simply to a new life and a new identity. . . .
>
> [But] the only possibility for a graceful experience of such a significant loss is through recognizing the potential that the crisis offers for a new perspective on one's individuality.[16]

As neighbors and as members of a Christian community we need to learn how to bring in the "food"—spiritual chicken soup for those on a dark journey. Assurance of pardon. Reminders that there is hope and life after this death. Resurrection. "Look around for a church that will help you meet your needs. I know of six separated ministers' wives in the church I go to. There may be more, I don't know. It's because it's an accepting church. That's what you need, not one that's going to be judgmental."

Some churches are better at that than others.

> The congregations that have been most effective in developing a ministry to the young ex-homemaker usually display a style of congregational life that is designed not to make anyone feel conspicuous. For example, the emphasis is on persons, not families. A fellowship or social event is called that, rather than "family night." . . . There is a strong New Testament emphasis on the love of God and on grace, rather than on guilt or judgment.[17]

As churches, we need to look closely at our attitudes toward single people of every variety.

We also need to let seminary students in on a little self-knowledge. "Why?" one woman practically shouted at me in anguish, "Why don't they *tell* students in seminary that there are *dangers* in this job. If there have been studies done on ministerial personality profiles, why don't they do some counseling around that?"

We need to share the learning these women have done. They can help us. They are frequently well educated ("A majority hold Bachelor of Arts degrees, thousands have their Masters, and many have PhDs"[18]), articulate, and faith-filled. They (along with others) could be teaching seminary students about what it means to live in a parsonage, about how to accept or refuse expectations, about the minister's own marriage.

Then, perhaps, these marriages will not come so often to the edge, and then over into divorce.

If a marriage does fail, these women also have advice on how to cope:

"Find a good counselor, friend, therapist; someone to talk to. (Another woman, preferably, to avoid gossip.)"

"Call on *all* your friends for help. One thing I've learned is that you can't talk about anything else when you're going through a divorce. You need enough friends to spread it around. One friend can't take it all."

"Separation counseling is a good thing. You need that."

"Find a church that is accepting."

"Get a *good* lawyer. There are many different types. Look for one who is both fair and who knows family law."

"Pray. When things are going better, you don't rely on God so much, and your life is *thinner,* somehow. I wouldn't want to go back to that trauma. But I miss that richness."

"Join a support group . . . at the 'Y' or wherever you can find one."

"Read. Betty Jane Wylie's book about widows [Beginnings] has the best practical advice for women living alone I've ever seen."*

Reflections

What does this all mean, in the end? For all of us, not just for the divorced minister's wife?

A look at those marriages which have broken down gives us a tool to evaluate our own marriages. What makes them tick? How could they be better? Gould expresses one criterion for a healthy marriage.

Perhaps the epidemic of divorce in the Western world is because our culture itself is in transition in its attitudes towards marriage: the static and growth concepts of marriage co-exist right now in our society. If one partner embraces the ideology of growth while the other tries to stop the change because of the belief that marriage should be static, then divorce is inevitable. But as the society creates more partners who believe in the growth concept of marriage, we may see not only a new stabilization of marriage but also a new form of the institution. Living through the rhythms of one's own growth against the pushes and pulls of a beloved partner over a lifetime creates a wonderfully dynamic relationship.[19]

When I asked one minister's wife what her divorce had meant to her theologically, she thought for a few minutes. "Well—it's the parable of the talents," she said slowly. "I had a lot of talents. Things I was good at, that were useful, that I enjoyed doing. But I was burying what I was called to be. Damned by not doing the things I was created to do. I simply was unable to deny my gifts any further."

Attempting to fit herself into a static marriage was a hopeless struggle, and she left. "Every time I prayed, I would see the vision of a backdoor. Finally I went through it."

Divorce is the alternate stage to the liberated marriage that Gould speaks of where two people "push and pull" against one another, accepting that they will grow at various rates, but that each must use his talents to the fullest.

If it comes to divorce, one has no other option but to cease projecting onto one's partner and learn to live out one's ambitions independently. It is a time of making it alone. It is a time of searching out the inward darkness, of descending into those dark parts, and getting to know them deeply.

It is good if that can be done within the marriage. If it cannot, it is good if the church can be supportive in this time of pain. Nothing less than the psychological counterpart of the Resurrection is necessary. It is our business as followers of Christ to be with the divorced person until that day.

V

The Two-Career Marriage

For as many of you as were baptized into Christ have put on
Christ. There is neither Jew nor Greek, there is neither slave
nor free, there is neither male nor female; for you are all one
in Christ Jesus.

—Galatians 3:28

The Two-Income Clergy Family

After liberation, what? A new stage. Slowly, I have
begun to make the mental shift from housewife to writer.
We are becoming a two-career couple—with kids.

That is not unusual for ministers' wives. According to a
1976 study of Episcopal clergy wives by Nancy Van Dyke
Platt and David M. Moss, more ministers' wives are
working outside the home than before.

While 50% of the women in this study [1976] were not
employed either full- or part-time, in 1962 75% of those in a
larger national study were not employed. Since other data
are relatively compatible, one factor in this difference may be

94

the change in opinion over employment for clergy wives. . . .

Although 79% of the study's respondents have professional training and skills, only 50% of them work full- or part-time. This figure is below the national average, which shows 70% of all women college graduates in the U.S. working at least part of the second half of their adult lives, i.e. ages 40-65. It is higher than national statistics, which show only one-third of all married women employed.

It is probable that as children reach school age, the need for additional income and savings to meet living expenses and college education savings sends many of the respondents back to work. [And] the return to a profession of her own provides additional satisfaction for the clergy wife.[1]

I asked my husband how it felt, having a wife who was a career woman.

"It means I have a happier wife," he said immediately. "And I'm proud, too. I *like* telling people my wife is a writer."

He grinned happily. I was suddenly terrified. This is how men must feel sometimes, I thought, if their wives depend on them for identity and status. What if I fail? How (I thought) could I ever face him—or anyone—again?

But my husband has his own identity quite securely, thanks. And thanks again, I couldn't carry that for him. I don't know how anyone can, but some do.

"It means friends outside the church, too," he went on. "That's a good thing." Yes—not that we don't love our friends within the church community; we do—dearly. But sometimes we need to come up against skepticism, and a different set of projections than the "minister" ones, even though none of us as a human is ever completely free of carrying an image.

"And I've learned a lot from you, lately, while you've been working on this book."

I beamed.

"Of course," he went on slowly, choosing his words, "it's harder to *relax* at home. There's always something to do, to hold up my end of the household chores. Sometimes my days are fourteen hours long. Then I don't feel like vacuuming."

This did not seem to be an appropriate moment for me to embark on a lecture about workaholism. I gritted my teeth and remained silent.

"We don't have as much time together as I'd like," he went on (or as I'd like, I thought to myself).

"But," he concluded cheerfully, "it's just good to see you so happy."

I *am* happy. I am beginning, as Gould describes it, to do the work of this time. I am thirty-six. I am making commitments to pursue something beyond the family, feeling my power.

That is what is crucial about the two-career marriage. Not so much the money (that's nice, though). Not so much an added dimension to my identity (although that's nice too). But getting in touch with my own strength.

> Entering the job market taps women's primitive competitive urge and the hunger for power, revenge and status that they had to deny as good little girls. . . . Once they no longer deny it as a part of their nature, they are free to entertain their own fully adult powers.[2]

My shark dream again. Powerful, primitive, and not to be denied.

> For some women this new sense of personal power allows them to let down their guard with their husbands and become better friends, sometimes even partners in work or in other shared activities. Rivalry and competition between

husband and wife disappear once they acknowledge that *he is no longer responsible for making her life work out.* They can enjoy their friendship as two independent, vulnerable human beings.[3] (Italics mine)

Gould does make it clear, however, that starting a career is not the only way to achieve this "return to strength."

To take back her power, a woman does not need to go to work. . . . For women who've lived in a traditional marriage until their mid-life decade, going back to work or starting a career is *only one way* to support and affirm their new sense of who they are. Some women pursue interests in politics or in social, cultural, or artistic endeavors; it matters only that women use their powers without reservation.[4] (Italics mine)

I have a friend who is now, in her thirties, at last developing her skills as a dancer. It involves two hours commuting, two full days a week, out of a busy life with three children. She is not doing it as a career, to earn money. She is simply "using her powers without reservation." It has precisely the same affirming effect on her sense of self as working would.

Problems

It is a joyous, frightening (What if I *do* fail?), but most of all affirming time. It has its pain, too, like every stage. There are problems. Witness the scenario below. It could take place in any two-career home where at least one spouse has heavy professional responsibilities.

He: Did I remember to tell you that I have a pastoral concerns meeting tomorrow night?

She: Tomorrow night is my teaching night, remember? So you get the sitter.

He: Oh, yeah. Sure, I just haven't had time to get to a phone.

She: (tentatively) Um. I'm still kind of mad about last week, by the way.

He: (unguarded, surprised) Last week? Mad?

She: The dishes. I was at work, and you didn't do the dishes. But you were at home. It was your turn.

He: (mentally still with the pastoral concerns meeting) Mm. Dishes.

She: They were still on the table when I came home from work.

He: (abruptly returning from the meeting) Oh! sorry, sorry, honey. I was up all Saturday night doing the sermon, and then Mrs. Clark was sick, and then we had the youth workshop on Monday and Tuesday, and then on Tuesday night I was so tired I just fell asleep after supper.

She: (sympathy and irritation struggling in her voice) I know. I know you must be tired. (irritation wins) But then the grease hardens on them, and I find them so hard to do in the morning, and who wants to do dishes in the morning anyway?

I could go on. But most of the issues I'd like to look at in this chapter on the two-career marriage are in this dialogue: lack of time, child care responsibilities, and division of household tasks.

Time

Time is an enormous issue in any two-career family. William Behrens of the Office of Support to Ministries of the American Lutheran Church puts it realistically. "The supply of time is equal for all persons. We each have all there is! The key is effective management of that same amount of time we all have available."[5]

Given that management of time is important, however, there is heavy pressure—especially on the clergy half of the couple—to try to put in forty-hour work days. True to the profile Jack Bloom described, he struggles to fulfill everyone's needs. "At the root of it all is the age old controversy over whether we earn God's love or whether it's an undeserved free gift. My head has known that God's love is free ever since I became a Christian. I have trouble translating that into living."[6]

One solution to the problems of time and child care, though, is to take advantage of the flexibility inherent in the minister's schedule. Industry is starting to use "flexible time." Clergy, to some extent, already have it.

> More than 6% of American employees solve timing problems like this [who takes Suzie to the dentist] by working for companies that give them some control over their working hours. Typically, flexible time employers set a core period during the middle of the day when everyone must be present. An employee then has the option of arriving or leaving within a wider range of hours.[7]

So if the clergy half of the couple has evening meetings four nights a week he might legitimately stay home a couple of mornings a week and look after the preschoolers while his wife does two half-day stints as a librarian.

Parenting

However, babysitters and making use of flexible time schedules is not the whole issue. The space one makes in the scheme of things for one's parenting function is important.

Burton L. White points out in his study of child development, *The First Three Years of Life,* how crucial parenting is.

> I have devoted my whole professional career to pursuing the question of how competent people get that way. On the basis of years of research, I am totally convinced that the first priority with respect to helping each child to reach his maximum level of competence is to do the best possible job in structuring his experience and opportunities during the first three years of life. Now, if I am totally convinced of that concept then it becomes painfully obvious to me, at least, that any other kind of job, be it formal or informal, working as an engineer somewhere, working as the president of a bank, working as a career professional in designing, or in the arts, *cannot really compete (in humanistic terms) with the job of helping a child make the most of his potential for a rich life.*[8] (Italics mine)

Behrens echoes that sentiment, "One's *primary responsibility* for the care of spouse and children must not be compromised in any individualistic pursuit of career development by either husband or wife"[9] (italics mine).

Both Dr. White and Behrens mention the possibility of two part-time jobs as a way to allow both parents to have their career in and out of the home. "Consider," says Behrens, "modeling a life style which does not require two full incomes."[10]

There is great reward in doing that sort of juggling, so that mother and father have some share in the parenting process. For the woman, there is the possibility of keeping in touch with her masculine side—the side that conducts meetings, speaks to large groups, and makes speeches. For the man, there is the possibility of getting in touch with the feminine within. Robert Raines describes this feeling.

"I am recognizing Mary now as my sister under the skin. The Mary in me is beginning to live . . . [and] when I allow the Mary in me to emerge, I am more able to be sensitive to the initiative of God."[11]

For him, this meant a new relationship with his own sister, and a beginning to the casting off of the subtle sexism with which our culture can infect us. In that culture, mothering has been considered a second-class activity; but as more and more men become involved in it, class distinctions disappear.

In our own family, we are struggling. To write this book, for example, I took occasional study leaves (at first with the baby along, as she was still being breastfed; there are some things men cannot do). I went to my parents' home, for three or four days at a time, leaving my husband and the older boys to cope.

They coped.

As a matter of fact they had a fine time. They made their own lunches, they cooked dinner, in the morning they got themselves out to work and to school. When I came home, the house was spotless.

"Territoriality"

I was delighted. To my surprise, I was even a tiny bit miffed, which showed me a dynamic that explains some of the difficulty men and women have with this issue. "Men married to working women in 1975 devoted only 9.7 hours to household labor while their wives put in 24.9." [But] to his surprise, Robinson discovered that working wives don't seem to mind the overload. Only 23% thought their husbands ought to do more. "It's territoriality," he says. "Just as many husbands feel reluctant to give up their

101

status as breadwinners, women cling to their identities as homemakers."[12]

So the shift in consciousness toward a marriage of two equal careers is gradual. It can be done, though; the important thing is that both halves of the couple retain their vision of ministry as a unity.

> Having made a commitment to one another, husband and wife seek to serve God not only as individuals but as a unity which God has joined together. It is incumbent then that in the two-income clergy family husband and wife will decide how they will serve God through their respective careers in concert. This means that *one's own view of serving as an individual will have to be tempered by the vision of serving in unity.* The couple may have to go through a process of determining priorities—not on the basis of any assumed greater importance of one vocation over another, but on the basis of what they judge to be the best ways for them to serve God individually *and as a unit* in and for the world.[13] (Italics mine)

A lot of things come together in that passage. First of all, one career is not more important than the other. So decisions about which career has priority cannot be based on the assumption, say, that the clergy half of the team "serves God" and hence comes first. That won't work.

The couple must reexamine some of the projections onto the clergy half of the couple. As a symbol-bearer for the faith, his vocation is enormously and rightfully important; just as the lawyer's vocation is important as a symbol of justice, and the politician's as a symbol of the democratic process.

But as a Christian, the vocation of the clergyperson in the marriage is not more important than that of the other Christian in the marriage. Christ's ministry may find expression in both. That is a tricky and extremely important issue. The idea that the "ministry" of the ordained clergy is somehow more valid, more *real* than the "ministry" of the nonordained Christian is both damaging and well-rooted in the thinking of people in many denominations.

The issue is further clouded by the limitations of language. In order to write this book, for example, I have had to use the term "minister" to refer to someone who is ordained. I have spoken of "the minister and his wife," as if she were not also a minister.

> . . . Christians everywhere seem to be realizing that it is important to make clear that *the basic use of the term "ministry" should be the generic use which refers to the ministry of Jesus Christ in which the whole church participates.*[14]

> During the Reformation era, Luther in particular transformed the concept of vocation . . . the wall of separation between "religious vocation" and "secular work" was torn down. Now, in his thinking, every person serves God through whatever "station" in life he or she finds himself/herself—whether that be in the ordained ministry, or whether it be in government service, the professions, trades, farming, labor. . . . There are no "higher" or "lower" orders of vocation.[15]

That leads us back to chapter 1 again. Just as a couple must search out their own values, under the discipline of the church, in terms of their *financial* stewardship, so they also have to dig deeply into their spiritual resources to discover the implications of their *vocational* stewardship.

Our basic connection is not with our status as ordained or lay members of the church. The basic connection is with God.

So both halves of a two-career couple must—*as a unit*—figure out the best way to serve. This is not easy. It involves making time for prayer and reflection (the time issue again).

That "time for prayer" also helps us deal with another problem. The scenario might continue like this:

He: Did you see this letter from Stu Brown?

She: (head bent over a battery of tests she's been arranging for her grade three remedial reading group) Mmm mm.

He: They need a minister, and you know, I have to think about it. They need what I'm good at. And we've been here twelve years. Maybe it's time . . .

She: (head no longer bent) What did you say?

He: We have to think about this.

She: But—I'm just getting this program to the point where it's working . . .

He: Yes. Well . . . we'll just have to talk about it, that's all.

The church's stress on mobility varies from denomination to denomination. But most churches consider themselves national in character, and that may mean being asked at some point to serve anywhere in the country. "We are ordained by the whole church," one minister explained to me, "and that means we have to serve anywhere in that church where there is a need. We are not ordained by one section of the church in one part of the country." This can create distinct conflicts in the two-career family.

Since the business world is being faced for the first

time with the same problems, it might be worthwhile to see how it is handling it—even though in business the problem might be lacking some of the dimensions of the problem of the marriage in which one member is ordained.

> The typical or traditional "solution" to these divergent needs [of two careers] has been to discourage women from any serious career pursuit. If the husband's career is viewed as more important, the wife will make the greater sacrifices, either by not working or by taking a series of dead-end jobs. Wives without careers are then free to follow their husbands from job to job, uprooting and nesting at the corporation's beck and call.[16]

That fits. One way that clergy families have solved this problem is for the wives to make a large investment in their husband's career, as "helpmate." Another way has been to have a fairly portable career, such as nursing or teaching used to be before the employment squeeze.

But both of these options are less and less available. The former because women's views about the importance of their vocational lives have changed so radically, the latter because of changing economic conditions. The nursing-teaching type jobs simply may not be available in the next location.

There are added complications coming. If the clergyman's wife is serious about her career, *she* may be asked to move. And there may not be a "call" for him in the new community.

How does business cope? "Couples," say Cathleen Maynard and Robert A. Zawacki in *Personnel Journal*, "have to be very creative and flexible—setting priorities, making choices and accepting trade-offs."[17] Some of their suggestions:

1. Take a balance sheet approach. Decide what works out best for each and for both. Compromise.
2. Alternate which career takes precedence with the idea that there will be cycles of opportunity.
3. Integrate careers by working full-time with spouse.
4. Reverse traditional roles. He becomes "househusband."
5. Commuter marriage.

Companies need to be creative and flexible too, Maynard suggests. Personnel managers "should recognize the changing composition of the work force and examine their personnel policies in the light of the increasing number of dual career couples."[18]

Principles from business often do not translate into church terms but some of these ideas might be worth examining. Alternating which career takes precedence, for example, is quite feasible for ministerial couples—although housing may become a problem if his contribution to the housing effort has been in the form of a manse; they are no longer eligible for that if he decides to be a househusband for a while.

On the other hand, the manse could be a decided advantage if the non-clergy part of the couple wishes to stay home and be the "enabler" for a while, instead of scuttling to help meet mortgage payments. The traditional marriage is increasingly a luxury that manse dwellers, unlike many other young couples, can still manage.

Becoming a company couple: the counterpart to this in the church is increasingly becoming an option as more and more women enter the ordained ministry. It is an almost ideal solution for the woman who has strong instincts to be a helpmate, but who otherwise might someday look around and notice that next door is a clergy couple—both ordained—who are doing exactly what she and her husband have been doing for years; only the other couple is getting paid for it.

There are no simple answers. Only pressures, sometimes conflicting demands, and different responsibilities, to be sorted out. The church as an institution may have to act as an employer (and ask the clergyman to move) at the same time that it is required to be the carrier of the faith that will enable the couple to come to a decision.

Perhaps Behrens should have the last word: "Neither role (that of husband or wife) is more important. Through marriage, husband and wife have become one (Mark 10:8). This means that . . . neither husband or wife is to claim greater importance for his or her means of serving God in the world."[19]

That helps me deal with the dilemma raised by my friend, the minister's wife. "My husband told me at the beginning of our marriage that his responsibility to the church came first. Before me, before any children we might have. He loved me very deeply, he said, but our family could have of him what the church could spare." No way.

> One can change occupations without sin; one may not without sin abrogate one's responsibilities as a husband or wife, father or mother. In any conflict between marriage and family commitments on the one hand, and occupational commitments on the other, one's basic responsibilities to marriage and family must be understood as primary. Married clergy should seek to model this priority.[20]

To that end, we need to have more career or life-decision retreats made easily available, so that people who are involved in decisions about career (especially where one of

107

the factors is one's commitment to the church) can get away and find some space and the spiritual resources with which to arrange that priority.

That leads us to the second part of this chapter. The "clergy couple." Read on.

The "Clergy Couple"

Some of the pioneering work in this kind of situation is being done by the two-clergy couple ("clergy couple" for the sake of convenience). Like those ministerial couples who are coping with the problem of divorce, those couples who are dealing with the issue of two ministers in one family have a great deal to teach the rest of us. There are an estimated one thousand clergy couples in North America. But the numbers are rising fast.

Many of the problems they face are not peculiar to them. The problems simply appear a little larger than life in their marriages. The mechanisms that they and the church develop to help can assist us all.

Besides, it is an intriguing issue for its own sake. The term "projection" pops up again. This book has looked at the question of why some men feel impelled to enter ministry. But why do some women marry men who become ministers? Perhaps it is because they have been able to fulfill some of their own needs by doing so. "It followed then, that in choosing a partner, one would be attracted to a person through whom one could experience, vicariously at least, *those aspects of one's own being that one could not live out conveniently in the world*"[21] (italics mine).

Before the ordination of women was a common practice

108

in many denominations, that was one solution. If you couldn't be a minister, you could marry one. As one former minister's wife confessed, "Our marriage held up so long because he was the only man I knew who would talk theology with me. I had actually thought about entering the ministry a long time ago. Before I met him. But I was actively discouraged by the seminary I approached from doing so."

But now many women are being ordained, in increasing numbers. And many ministers' wives—myself included—feel a pull to join them. It is a healthy opportunity to recall some of the ambitions and talents that may have been lived vicariously through the clergy half of the marriage.

Problems

What are the problems faced by the two-clergy marriage, problems that we all might identify with?

Witness another scenario, this time between a husband and wife who are both ordained.

She: Have you seen that paper from the Alban Institute? The one about moving ministers? I forget what the title is.

He: Uh-huh. I think it's in my files somewhere. I'll get it when I go down to the church tomorrow.

She: Aagh! I need it tonight. I've been looking all day . . .

He: Oh, sure. Well, while I'm down there, I could finish those prayers for Sunday.

First child:	You going to watch "The Muppets" with us tonight, Daddy?
He:	I sure don't want to miss "The Muppets!"
She:	. . . the paper?
Second child:	Want to play baseball after supper, Mum? Dad?
She:	Gee, I have that workshop to get ready for.
First child:	You're *not* going to miss Miss Piggy!
He:	I wish I could remember where I *put* that paper . . . is it in the desk here at home? Your milk, Susie!
She:	Oh, damn!
Third child (baby):	Milk a' gone!

First and second child vanish from table.

| He: | *(wiping up milk)* Did you take a message for me from Mrs. Clark? |
| She: | It's on the upstairs phone, sorry. What do you think she might do? |

He and she embark on an animated conversation about Mrs. Clark. The baby plays happily in a small puddle of spilled milk Daddy missed, and the older children are not heard of again except for an occasional bleat from the television set.

That scenario illustrates what Kenneth Mitchell, Dean of the University of Dubuque Theological Seminary, calls conflation. "Those problems which arise when work concerns illicitly dominate and intrude upon family and individual life and vice versa."

> Clergy couples . . . may fail to keep a sufficient line of demarcation between work and individual or family areas. The seductive temptation for this kind of conflation of course lies in the fact that on occasion there arise either work or family issues which are difficult to deal with.[22]

He: Do you think the children might be watching too much TV? I'm a bit concerned about it.

She: Umm-hmm. What should we do, do you think?

He: I should be playing with them more.

She: I should too.

(Long pause)

He: But I'm too tired right now.

She: Maybe what Mrs. Clark should look into is some help from . . .

> It is particularly at such times that the clergy couple may choose to avoid the real problems at hand by simply switching the topic of conversation. Clergy couples clearly need to be on the look out for instances of this kind of conflation. Conflation may create some needed space and distance as significant problems are broached. [But] It can have devasting consequences if it is used as a device for the complete avoidance of problems which genuinely require a direct and open hearing.[23]

111

Mitchell also describes an amorphous creature lurking in the nuclear family known as "the undifferentiated family ego mass," the pressure the family itself places on each person in it to subscribe wholeheartedly to the dominant family value system.

Both parents (to take one example) might strongly value hard work. The children will also be heavily influenced by the work ethic. Of course, they may—they will *have* to—struggle against this as they mature and begin to diassociate themselves from the family mass. They will need to do the work of adolescence—pulling away from the family and discovering who they are and what their values are—before they develop their own family, with its own mass.

Both parents and children may find that necessary rebellion difficult to cope with in any family. But in a home where the parents share a rather consuming vocation, such as the ministry, that difficulty in pulling away may be overwhelming.

> The results of this conflation for the lives of the children may be profound if not potentially disastrous. When family life becomes too much dominated by work and church issues, *there is clear and present risk that the children involved will not receive the sheer amount of individual and undiluted attention and care that is required for the normal development of individual identity and a positive self image.* . . . Children in such homes are often forced to unheroically comply with the dominant professional and valuational thrust of the family, or to establish their individuality through the avenue of a total revolt from the family of origin.[24] (Italics mine)

If the latter is the case, at least the work of establishing an identity will be done. But the child as an adult may then find him or herself cut off from his/her faith at a time of crisis, unable to return to it because that would entail the giving up of the hard-won independence. And if the former is the case, the child may have to postpone his/her identity-building until well into the adult years, when it is much more difficult. (See Robert Raines' moving account of this in *Going Home*.)

Another difficulty with the family ego mass and the couple who are both deeply involved in their mutual work is that one member of the couple may change. According to the work Gould, Sheehy, and Levinson have done, one member *will* change, at a different time than the other. The midlife crisis, for example, has to come sometime.

> While the dilemma for this decade [age 35-54] is the search for authenticity, the work is to move through a disassembling to a renewal. What is disassembling is that narrow self we have thus far put together in a form tailored to please the culture and other people.
> . . . By allowing this dis-integration, by taking in our suppressed and even our unwanted parts, each of us prepares at the gut level for the reintegration of an identity that is truly our own.[25]

So the couple in our example who have uncritically made work a god may suddenly find that one of them has "disassembled" that self-image and taken up long canoe trips, or dancing, or sitting watching the birds. One of them may decide that it is time to opt out of the parish ministry for a while. But "precisely to the degree that the couple has *uncritically* formed an undifferentiated family ego mass will such fundamental changes in either party be the source of potentially explosive problems."

> If the proper distinction and differentiation between marriage and ministry has not been maintained, the decision

of one to leave the ministry may well threaten to destroy either the marriage or the other's ministerial self understanding. Or a change in personality or values may rudely rock the marital ship as well as call into question the style if not the possibility of ministerial endeavours.[26]

Every family, Mitchell goes on to explain, has this monster at work in it. It is not an unfriendly beast, this "undifferentiated family ego mass," even though it has a long title. It is just that it tends to breathe fire if it is not watched. And when both parties in a marriage are wrapped up in a vocation that is as absorbing as ministry, and as filled with benevolent intentions, then the dragon can sleep in their shadows and mature unnoticed, until the day he wakes up and burns down the house *and* the marriage with his first good yawn.

Mitchell describes these elements and others (competition, for example) as they are found in the lives of couples in which husband and wife are both ordained. But they are present in other homes, too, especially those in which the spouse has a deep involvement with and sympathy for her husband's ministry. In the home where husband and wife take an active part in church life, the temptation to have the profession of ministry dominate everything else in the family is there. In this area we can all learn from clergy couples.

How can we avoid such problems? They confront all of us, not just clergy couples.

It may mean deliberately choosing to have *some* friends who are outside your church. That lessens the temptation to talk shop, and gives the children a chance to discover other models than the ministerial one.

It may mean deliberately organizing a separate support group for each half of the couple, so that the dinner hour is not marked by constant efforts by each spouse to give the other badly needed "ventilation time" about his or her efforts and frustrations.

It may mean being careful to arrange time as a couple to discuss work-type problems away from the children. Save some time for each person to be treated as an individual—the dinner hour, a fishing trip, "The Muppets." And a chance for a *couple* to have time that is uncontaminated by church issues—at a movie, on a hiking trip, and most of all in the bedroom. Bed is no place to be joined by the ghost of the chairman of the board, or the spiritual presence of the current counselee.

Most of all, it means struggling to find your own time as an individual away from your work—whether it is being helpmate or enabler or liberated woman who carries a briefcase or career woman. ". . . I remembered some feelings from years ago, [I had had at] an event of some sort in New York where I was working. We were asked to say who we were without reference to our jobs. I couldn't do it."[27]

If that happens to you or your husband, it is a sure sign that you need to see yourself in other ways than minister or minister's wife or career woman. Retreat time, maybe. Or a holiday.

Reflections

What does it mean, then, as a woman, to have a career of one's own, to be partly helpmate, partly enabler, mostly liberated? It means that at last I can understand how my husband feels. "There is neither male nor female," St. Paul says. "You are all one in Christ." The two-career marriage gives us a unique opportunity to discover the dimensions of the other sex within us—to take on the task of the partner, share it, and ease his burden at the same time that your own is eased.

When the husband cuddles the baby, changes the diapers, embarks distrustfully on his first encounter with the washing machine and is present to the small person who has scraped a knee, he is not just overturning traditional patterns; he is discovering new areas within himself. He is learning the woman's magic that hears the words the six-month-old can't say yet and heals the knee that belongs to someone who is afraid he will never learn to ride a bike.

When the wife has to organize her day around a transit strike for the first time or has to deal rationally with the conflict with the co-worker at the office or discovers that she *has* the skill to persuade a meeting to move in one direction or another, she is not just changing positions from housewife to career woman. She is growing up to be a big strong "man," while remaining a woman. We do not lose our other side when we change roles, or experiment with a new one. We keep it.

I watched my oldest son and his father learning how to make croissants the other day. The kitchen was dusted with flour, and so were they. They were excited. The rising of the dough, the rolling, the buttering and baking, the miracle of the yeast was wonderful to them.

But I had not forgotten how it felt, even though I had a deadline to meet and couldn't make croissants, too. I knew the moment when the dough becomes elastic in your hands, and the smooth, smooth feel of the ball of bread when it is at last ready to be tucked away in the big bowl to rise. I had not forgotten. I shall never forget. It is a part of me.

The sharing of the household tasks, the sharing in the support of the family is a way to "become one" in St. Paul's sense—both as an individual and as a couple. The masculine and feminine in the psyche, searching for each other throughout adolescence and early adulthood, can begin to discover one another at last.

Gould puts it another way.

Both of us are driven to rework our old concepts of the male and female aspects of ourselves. Underneath the old conspiracies, at mid-life we are negotiating to find room for our newly forming selves.

To oversimplify it, as men we're striving for release from our stereotyped masculinity and opening ourselves up to need, uncertainty, anxiety, and ambiguity. As women we're striving for release from our sterotyped femininity and taking on new strengths, autonomy, freedom, novelty and self-confidence.[28]

Of course being both is not an easy job. It is even dangerous. What if I *should* forget how to hear the baby talking? What if this new strength should take me over? What then?

I had a dream, just as I was coming to the end of this book. It is a dream I can share, perhaps, with other women who are trying to hold it all together: the family and the career, the feminine and the masculine. It is a suitable story with which to close. I began to drive away from home in a wagon pulled by a big strong horse. Jim (my husband) shouted, "It's hard to control!"

I said, "I don't care!" and flew along (I *was* in control, too) with the baby in the wagon crying, and me on the horse, and Jim in the distance behind, shouting to be careful.

Finally I got down off the horse and held its head tightly

117

and walked along, half on my knees and half-dragged. But I *knew* I was in control so far, and I was happy with my strength.

I was being warned. The baby (a girl) was crying. The gentle, feminine part of me was resisting (with good reason) the bouncing ride she was being exposed to.

But there is joy in the dream, too. I was just barely in control. But I *was* managing. I *could* do it.

And I will not forget to cuddle the baby. Someday I am going to dream that dream again, and it will be better. I will ride along with that girl-child secure and happy beside me; she will have one rein, and I will have the other. The ride will be smooth and comfortable. Jim and the boys will wave proudly as we go by. Or perhaps they will jump on too. And the big horse will be *very* strong, and *very* obedient.

There is lots of room in the wagon. Welcome aboard, anyone else who wants to come.

Notes

Introduction

1. Gail Sheehy, *Passages: Predictable Crises of Adult Life* (New York: Bantam, 1977), p. 31.
2. United Church of Canada, "The Report of Project Ministry," 1980, p. 9.
3. William Behrens, "The Two-Income Clergy Family" (Office of Support to Ministries, the American Lutheran Church), unpublished, p. 6.

I. The Helpmate

1. Donna Sinclair, "A Town of a Reddish Colour," *The United Church Observer*, July, 1970, p. 16.
2. *Ibid.*
3. Lucille Lavender, *They Cry Too* (New York: Hawthorne, 1976), p. 74.
4. William Presnell, "The Minister's Own Marriage," *Pastoral Psychology*, Summer, 1977, p. 274.
5. *Ibid.*, p. 275.
6. Robert Kemper, "Patterns of Ministry," *The Christian Century*, May, 1980, p. 26.

7. Presnell, "The Minister's Own Marriage," p. 278.
8. Kemper, "Patterns of Ministry," p. 26.
9. Presnell, "The Minister's Own Marriage," p. 278.
10. *Ibid.*, p. 277.
11. Manfred Holck, Jr., "What Is Clergy Compensation?" *The Christian Ministry*, September, 1975, p. 20.
12. Arthur Bell, "Your Salary—Up or Down?" *The Christian Ministry*, March, 1974, p. 6.
13. Roger Gould, *Transformations: Growth and Change in Adult Life* (New York: Simon & Schuster, 1978), p. 76.
14. Robert Rankin, "The Ministerial Calling and the Minister's Wife," *Pastoral Psychology*, September, 1960, p. 17.
15. *Ibid.*
16. Gould, *Transformations*, p. 10.
17. Patricia Clarke, "Manse and Wife," *The United Church Observer*, April, 1972, p. 31.

II. The Enabler

1. Gould, *Transformations*, p. 135.
2. *Ibid.*, p. 101.
3. Henri Nouwen, *Reaching Out* (Garden City, N.Y.: Doubleday, 1975), p. 28.
4. *Ibid.*, p. 30.
5. *Ibid.*, p. 36.
6. Gould, *Transformations*, p. 135.
7. John Ordway, "Transference Reactions in Parishioners," *The Journal of Pastoral Care*, March, 1970, p. 56.
8. James E. Davison, "On Transference," *Pastoral Psychology*, April, 1971, p. 26.
9. John Ordway, "Transference Reactions in Parishioners," p. 59.
10. Nathaniel S. Lehrman, "The Normality of Sexual Feelings in Pastoral Counselling," *Pastoral Psychology*, June, 1960, p. 4.
11. Charles Rassieur, *The Problem Clergymen Don't Talk About* (Philadelphia: Westminster Press, 1976), p. 61.
12. *Ibid.*, p. 146.
13. James Hillman, *Insearch: Psychology and Religion* (New York: Scribner's, 1967), p. 35.
14. *Ibid.*, p. 36.
15. Gould, *Transformations*, p. 182.

III. The Liberated Woman

1. Gould, *Transformations*, p. 163.
2. Esther Harding, *The "I" and the "Not-I"* (Princeton: Princeton University Press, Bollingen Series, 1965), p. 74.
3. Irene Claremont de Castillejo, *Knowing Woman* (New York: Harper & Row, 1973), p. 30.
4. *Ibid.*, p. 101.
5. Bruce Reed, *The Dynamics of Religion* (London: Darton, Longman and Todd, 1978), p. 172.
6. David K. Switzer, "The Minister as Pastor and Person," *Pastoral Psychology*, Fall, 1975, p. 56.
7. *Ibid.*, p. 57.
8. *Ibid.*, p. 58.
9. Harding, *The "I" and the "Not-I*," p. 73.
10. "Despite Appearances, Ministers' Wives Are Only Human," pamphlet (Minneapolis, Minn.: Ministers Life and Casualty Union).
11. Harding, *The "I" and the "Not-I*," p. 78.
12. Hillman, *Insearch*, p. 76.
13. *Ibid.*, p. 77.
14. Harding, *The "I" and the "Not-I*," p. 79.
15. *Ibid.*, p. 78.
16. Philip Marchand, "How Family Therapy Heals Hidden Conflicts in the Home," *Chatelaine*, June, 1980, p. 110.
17. Gould, *Transformations*, p. 49.
18. Robert Raines, *Going Home* (New York: Harper & Row, 1979), p. 7.
19. *Ibid.*, pp. 33, 34.
20. Gould, *Transformations*, p. 153.
21. Harding, *The "I" and the "Not-I*," p. 98.

IV. Divorce and the Minister's Wife

1. Lucille Lavender, *They Cry Too*, p. 97.
2. Lyle E. Schaller, "The Young Ex-homemaker," *The Parish Paper*, pamphlet (Richmond, Ind.: Yokefellow Institute), October, 1979.
3. Ellen Goodman, *Turning Points* (New York: Fawcett Columbine, 1979), p. 168.
4. William Douglas, *Ministers' Wives* (New York: Harper & Row, 1965), p. 2. (From Anon., "Hints for a Clergyman's Wife.")
5. Morton and Bernice Hunt, *The Divorce Experience* (New York: McGraw-Hill, 1977), p. 20.

6. Jack H. Bloom, "Who Become Clergymen?" *Journal of Religion and Health*, January, 1971, p. 53.
7. *Ibid.*, p. 65.
8. *Ibid.*, p. 64.
9. *Ibid.*, p. 63.
10. Anon., "My Church Has Let Me Down," *The United Church Observer*, October, 1975, p. 29.
11. *Ibid.*, p. 30.
12. Vidal S. Clay, "Where Are the Neighbors Bringing in Food?" *Pilgrimage: The Journal of Pastoral Psychotherapy*, Summer, 1975, p. 43.
13. Anon., "My Church Has Let Me Down," p. 30. Iris Murdoch is an Alberta ex-ranchwife who, in 1976 (a year after this article was written) *was* finally—after eight years of fighting in the courts—awarded a divorce settlement of $65,000 by the Supreme Court of Alberta. (It was only 12% of her former husband's property and assets, even though she had worked side by side with him doing equal amounts of heavy labor, to build up the ranch.)
14. Tom York, "Divorce," *The United Church Observer*, January, 1980, p. 35.
15. Clay, "Where Are the Neighbors Bringing in Food?" p. 36.
16. Penelope Washbourne, *Becoming Woman* (New York: Harper & Row, 1977), p. 71.
17. Schaller, "The Young Ex-homemaker."
18. Lavender, *They Cry Too*, p. 84.
19. Gould, *Transformations*, p. 324.

Note: Betty Jane Wylie, *Beginnings* (Toronto: McClelland and Stewart, 1977) is useful reading for the suddenly single, even though her book is for widows.

V. The Two-Career Marriage

1. Nancy Van Dyke Platt and David M. Moss, "Self-Perceptive Dispositions of Episcopal Clergy Wives," *Journal of Religion and Health*, July, 1976, pp. 195, 196.
2. Gould, *Transformations*, p. 259.
3. *Ibid.*, p. 260.
4. *Ibid.*, p. 265.
5. Behrens, "The Two-Income Clergy Family," p. 10.
6. Ralph Milton, "Confessions of a Workaholic," *The United Church Observer*, May, 1980, p. 27.

7. Marlys Harris, "Keeping a Working Marriage Working," *Money*, January, 1979, p. 46.
8. Burton L. White, *The First Three Years of Life* (Englewood Cliffs, N.J.: Prentice-Hall, 1975), p. 264.
9. Behrens, "The Two-Income Clergy Family," p. 15.
10. *Ibid.*
11. Robert Raines, *Going Home*, p. 89.
12. Harris, "Keeping a Working Marriage Working," p. 47.
13. Behrens, "The Two-Income Clergy Family," p. 7.
14. "The Report of Project Ministry," p. 8.
15. Behrens, "The Two-Income Clergy Family," p. 4.
16. Cathleen Maynard and Robert Zawicki, "Mobility and the Dual Career Couple," *Personnel Journal*, July, 1979, p. 468.
17. *Ibid.*, p. 470.
18. *Ibid.*, p. 471.
19. Behrens, "The Two-Income Clergy Family," p. 6.
20. *Ibid.*
21. June Singer, *Androgyny: Towards a New Theory of Sexuality* (Garden City, N.Y.: Anchor/Doubleday, 1977), p. 265.
22. Nancy Jo von Lackum and John P. von Lackum III, "Clergy Couples: A Report on Clergy Couples and the Ecumenical Clergy Couples Consultation, Mason, Ohio," National Council of Churches of Christ, 415 Riverside Dr., Room 770, New York, N.Y, p. 29.
23. *Ibid.*
24. *Ibid.*, p. 31.
25. Sheehy, *Passages*, p. 361.
26. von Lackum, "Clergy Couples," p. 28.
27. Milton, "Confessions of a Workaholic," p. 28.
28. Gould, *Transformations*, p. 278.

Bibliography

Behrens, William C. "The Two-Income Clergy Family." A paper for study by staff, Office of Support to Ministries, the American Lutheran Church.

de Castillejo, Irene Claremont. *Knowing Woman*. New York: Harper & Row, 1974.

Faraday, Ann. *The Dream Game*. New York: Harper & Row, 1974.

Goodman, Ellen. *Turning Points*. New York: Fawcett Columbine, 1979.

Gould, Roger. *Transformations: Growth and Change in Adult Life.* New York: Simon & Schuster, 1978.

Harding, Esther. *The "I" and the "Not-I."* Princeton University Press, (Bollingen Series), 1965.

von Lackum, Nancy Jo and von Lackum, John P., III. "Clergy Couples: A Report on Clergy Couples and the Ecumenical Clergy Couples Consultation, Mason, Ohio." National Council of Churches of Christ, 415 Riverside Drive, Room 770, New York, N.Y. 10027.

Nouwen, Henri. *Reaching Out*. Garden City, N.Y.: Doubleday and Co., 1975.

Raines, Robert. *Going Home*. New York: Harper & Row, 1979.

Sheehy, Gail. *Passages: Predictable Crises of Adult Life.* New York: Bantam, 1977.

The United Church of Canada. "The Report of Project Ministry." 85 St. Clair Ave., East, Toronto, Ontario M4T 1M8.

Washbourne, Penelope. *Becoming Woman.* New York: Harper & Row, 1977.